GETTING MORE VISI[TORS TO YOUR]
WEBSITE in 90 MINUTES

For a complete list of Management Books 2000 titles,
visit our web-site on http://www.mb2000.com

> The original idea for the 'In Ninety Minutes' series was presented to the publishers by Graham Willmott, author of 'Forget Debt in Ninety Minutes'. Thanks are due to him for suggesting what has become a major series to help business people, entrepreneurs, managers, supervisors and others to greatly improve their personal performance, after just a short period of study.

Titles in the original 'in Ninety Minutes' series include:

Forget Debt in 90 Minutes, Understand Accounts in 90 Minutes
Working Together in 90 Minutes, Supply Chain in 90 Minutes
Practical Negotiating in 90 Minutes, Faster Promotion in 90 Minutes
Find That Job in 90 Minutes, Become a Meeting Anarchist in 90 Minutes
Telling People in 90 Minutes, Strengths Coaching in 90 Minutes
Perfect CVs in 90 Minutes, Networking in 90 Minutes
Payroll in 90 Minutes, 25 Management Techniques in 90 Minutes
Budgeting in 90 Minutes, Active Learning in 90 Minutes

The series editor is James Alexander

> This new series of IT-focused 'in 90 Minutes' books will help readers travel through the sometimes confusing and esoteric world of Information Technology with greater ease and comprehension. The publishers acknowledge the help and guidance given by Martin Bailey, the author of this volume, in setting a great standard for the new series.

Titles in the 'IT in Ninety Minutes' series include:

Get More Visitors to Your Website in 90 Minutes
Building a Website Using a CMS in 90 Minutes
Think You Want a Website? in 90 Minutes
  ... others will be added as the series progresses

Submissions of possible titles for this series or for management books in general will be welcome. MB2000 are always keen to discuss possible new works that might be added to their extensive list of books for people who mean business.

GETTING MORE VISITORS to your WEBSITE in 90 Minutes

A guide to optimising your website and marketing strategies to generate more targeted visitors to your web site.

Martin Bailey

2000

Copyright © Martin Bailey 2006

All rights reserved. No part of this publication may be reproduced, stored in a retrieval system, or transmitted in any form or by any means, electronic, mechanical, photocopying, recording, or otherwise without the prior permission of the publishers.

First published in 2006 by Management Books 2000 Ltd
Forge House, Limes Road
Kemble, Cirencester
Gloucestershire, GL7 6AD, UK
Tel: 0044 (0) 1285 771441
Fax: 0044 (0) 1285 771055
E-mail: info@mb2000.com
Web: www.mb2000.com

Printed and bound in Great Britain by 4edge Ltd of Hockley, Essex –
www.4edge.co.uk

This book is sold subject to the condition that it shall not, by way of trade or otherwise, be lent, resold, hired out, or otherwise circulated without the publisher's prior consent in any form of binding or cover other than that in which it is published and without a similar condition including this condition being imposed upon the subsequent purchaser.

British Library Cataloguing in Publication Data is available

ISBN 1-85252-XXX-X

Contents

Introduction	7
1. Overview of Search Engines	9
2. Content is King	15
3. Finding the Right Keywords	21
4. Adding Meta Tags to Your Site	27
5. Streamlining Your HTML Code	33
6. Optimising Your Site for Your Keywords	41
7. Building Site Maps	49
8. Validating Your Web Code	55
9. Getting Links to Your Site	65
10. Using Content from Other Websites	73
11. Submitting Your Site to Search Engines	79
12. Tracking Your Effectiveness Through Web Statistics	83
13. Offline Promotion	87
Appendix 1: Quick Checklist	93
Appendix 2: Google's Most Loved and Hated SEO Tricks	95
Appendix 3 – The Web Promoter's Software Arsenal	97
Appendix 4 – Useful Sites	99
Glossary of Terms	101
Index	104

Introduction

'If you build it, they will come,' may have worked for Kevin Costner in *Field of Dreams*, but it doesn't necessarily work for the Internet. Companies spend thousands on web design only for their site to rot in cyberspace with few visitors ever finding it.

This book addresses many of the common mistakes that people make when trying to promote their online presence. While it predominantly focuses on search engine optimisation, there are also many tricks you can use on your site to make it easier to use. Enriching the amount of information available, the user experience and the accessibility for those with disabilities all play a part in making your place on the Internet an altogether more pleasant place to be.

A website should be the first place your customers want to look for information, not the last. In 90 minutes, with the help of this book, you will have a much better understanding of the changes you will need to make to your site to make it easier to find and use.

1. Overview of search engines

The Internet has forced us to interact with people and businesses in a very different way compared to only a decade ago. Previously we would go to a shop selling a product we desire, make a purchase and go home. This purchase would generally be made simpler by the product being on a shelf or aisle dedicated to similar products, with perhaps a store guide or staff member on-hand to help. With the Internet it's a whole different ball game – you have a web browser, but where do you start? Enter the search engine.

A brief history
The first search tool, known as 'Archie' was created in 1990, quickly followed by 'Gopher' in 1991. The first 'robot' – a program that automatically traverses the web's hypertext structure by reviewing documents and all subsequently linked documents that are referenced – was written in 1993. The first search engine – Excite – was unleashed the same year. It used statistical analysis of word relationships to aid in the search process. A plethora of engines sprang up in quick succession after this – Galaxy, Yahoo, Lycos, Altavista, WebCrawler, Northern Light and Infoseek to name but a few. Each used different methods of searching and analysing data to provide its results, promising more accuracy. The 'daddy' of search engines – Google – was launched in 1997. It used inbound links to rank sites, meaning that the more links a site had to it (relevant to the search term being used!), the more popular it must be, thus ranking it more highly. How Google ranks sites is a closely guarded secret.

What is a search engine?
In its simplest form it is a tool to allow users to search for pages on the Internet containing information on a specific subject, using relevant keywords. The results are sorted by the most relevant, based on the user's keywords. It is the ranking of these results that this entire book is dedicated to.

Everyone wants that number one position, but let's start by being realistic – don't expect to implement the recommendations from this book and get first place rankings overnight. Indeed, you may never reach number one – if you get on the first page of results for your top keywords, you'll be doing well, and this also depends on how saturated your market is already. Don't be too disheartened though, as there are plenty of small changes you can make to your site that can make a significant difference in your search engine placement, which can only have a positive effect on your business.

Understanding how search engines work is the fundamental first step in understanding the changes that you need to make to your site. This is in order for (a) search engines to be able to access all of your content, and (b) for your content to be optimised for your specific industry, and the terms that your prospects are likely to use. Remember that the search engine is simply a tool used by real people.

Search engines can provide much more information than just links to relevant websites. They can also locate news, maps, images, reviews, help to compare prices, and even find if there have been any reported problems with the product or the manufacturer. Type 'books' into Google and you can expect in excess of 1.3 billion results, but refine it to 'books, marketing' and it is whittled down to a mere 104 million. Narrow it down further to your country (e.g. select 'Pages from the UK') and it drops dramatically to 6.7 million. Add in 'Martin Bailey' to the search phrase and it plummets to 134,000. While this is still a mammoth amount of content, the chance that the right page will be at the top is much greater. People are starting to get savvy to the Internet and how it requires them to think if they are to retrieve the information they want quickly, so you would do well to keep this in mind whenever you are writing content for your site – we'll cover this in detail in the next chapter.

Search engine types
In addition to 'standard' search engines, there are others that need to be recognised:

- PPC, or Pay per Click search engines (such as Overture)
- Directories, which are generally edited by humans, and smaller than their electronically populated search engine counterparts. They often also cover niche markets
- Meta search engines, which recompile search results from other search engines and directories

Generally, if you get into the main search engines, then half the battle is won, as many other sites feed off or are powered by these goliaths. And there is one thing that all search engines feed on and rank by – your content! Tailoring your content to your users may sound like commonsense but you will be surprised how many sites fall foul of this simple rule.

The major search engines are:

- **Google** – currently handles over 50% of all searches

Overview of Search Engines

- **Yahoo**
- **Teoma**
- **MSN**

There are several others that are still considered major players, although altogether they probably account for less of the overall number of searches than Google, most of which are powered by the above listed engines.

- **AllTheWeb** – Scandinavian born competitor to Google used on many other sites and powered from the Yahoo! Search index.
- **AltaVista** – One of the first major players in the search industry, also powered from the Yahoo! Search index.
- **AOL** – Major web portal powered by Google.
- **Ask Jeeves** – Popular search site powered by Teoma. Ask Jeeves also owns Teoma and several other portal sites.
- **Earthlink** – Powered by Google.
- **Excite** – Web portal who's meta search engine results are powered by InfoSpace.
- **GigaBlast**.
- **Go** – Disney's web portal, powered by Google.
- **HotBot** – search engine originally launched with Inktomi.
- **InfoSpace** – website which powers many major meta search engines.
- **Inktomi** – Search database powering MSN and many smaller search sites.
- **LookSmart** – Pay per click search provider.
- **Lycos** – Uses LookSmart / Inktomi results.
- **Netscape** – Web portal owned by AOL which uses Google results
- **Overture** – One of the most powerful PPC search engines in the world.
- **WiseNut** – Search engine purchased by LookSmart, provides backfeed search results to LookSmart.

Many factors affect your site's rankings, some of which you have control over and some of which you don't. For example, Google will rank a site higher if the domain has been in use for a long time, or even if a specific

Getting More Visitors to Your Website in 90 Minutes

page filename has been in use a long time but is updated frequently. A new site would automatically not qualify for these two attributes by default, but that does not necessarily mean it will not rank highly if other factors come into play. Note that you can also optimise different pages to appeal to different search engines.

Even your domain name can work in your favour – choose a domain that has a relevant keyword in and this could dramatically increase your chances of getting closer to the all-important single-digit ranking. It may be worth buying an alternative domain name to your company name and promote this. Two excellent examples in the UK are DIY firm B&Q, whose domain is www.diy.com and high street chemist Boots, at www.wellbeing.com.

Where your site is hosted can have an effect on your rankings, as search engines can trace the site's location via its IP address. Therefore if the US is a big market for you it would be important to host with an American ISP.

Finally, don't believe anyone that can guarantee you first placement in the search engine for a top-ranking keyword or key phrase. No-one can guarantee this in engines such as Google, so you might simply be paying over the odds to be placed in a PPC engine, or, worst still being optimised for the wrong search terms. Anyone can get first page ranking for an obscure phrase containing eight keywords. There is no 'black art' to making a site search engine friendly, and in the following chapters we'll discuss what you can do – generally for free – to get listed. More importantly you'll learn what not to do, in order to avoid being blacklisted.

Our journey will start by looking at your existing content along with ideas for creating more pages. Next we'll discuss the importance of choosing the key words that users are likely to use. The next few chapters delve into your web pages, showing how you can apply your chosen keywords, add meta tags and a site map, and then cleaning up and validating your code. Once your pages are optimized, it is then a case of advising the search engines and getting other quality links into your site. Finally we will cover ways of monitoring your success and using methods outside of the Internet to promote your site further.

Overview of Search Engines

> **Summary**
>
> Before you can optimise your site for search engines you need to understand what they are and how they work. As you gain a better knowledge in this area you will naturally write content that is more optimised.

2. Content is King

It may sound like an obvious statement, but you need to ensure that you have enough relevant text on your website. The old adage of 'content is king' is still very true today. Even if you build and promote a site following all the advice in this book to the letter, you will not get good rankings if the content that the search engines eventually harvest does not merit their attention.

Let's be clear about what we mean by content – TEXT. Text, text and more text. And then some more... By all means add in images to your site. Add in Flash media as well if you wish, but it is text that search engines identify and rank against.

You may think that you cannot say much about your product or service other than what perhaps appears on your current literature, but there are ways around this. You don't have to necessarily just expand on what is written; it's more a case of writing content that compliments it. For example if you have a technical product why not write a technical article on the industry it serves? (This could also double as a good article that you could provide to a magazine – most of them love receiving quality content that is not a pure product plug). Case studies are another way of not only generating regular content for your website, but also regular PR content.

Online Discussion Forums

Online forums, also known as bulletin boards not only provide a useful place for your customers and prospects to discuss issues and ideas but also put content generation to the masses, although watch out as these are open to abuse (from disgruntled customers or competitors). There are plenty of free and highly customisable forum applications available, one excellent example being phpBB (www.phpbb.com). All you need is web space that supports PHP scripting and a mySQL database (available from under £100 per year from many hosts). Installation is relatively straightforward – just download the software from their website, unzip the files, upload them to your web space and then run through the online setup wizard. Once installed you can then configure the site to suit your needs – this includes multi-lingual support, design template modification, forum moderation (validating user's messages before placing them live) and setting various access levels for different users. The system automates many processes,

Getting More Visitors to Your Website in 90 Minutes

including registration emails, lost passwords, emailing updates to users etc, and is an excellent way to add a 'pulse' to your site. Users that do abuse the system can also be banned.

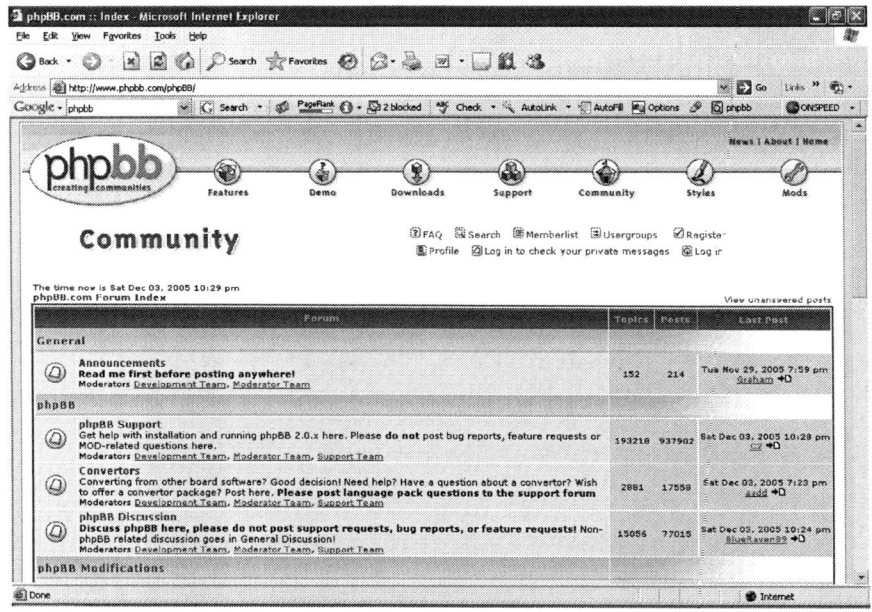

2.1. Adding a discussion group can be like adding a pulse to your site

If you have a busy site, your site lends itself to a forum and if you have the resources (and the will!) to regularly monitor it then you will hopefully find that it is quickly filled with posts from users that contain rich and relevant content. When people search for rather obscure combinations of keywords relating to your product/industry, then you stand a better chance of having your site listed. Google also likes larger sites, so the more pages your forum generates the better.

When and why not to include a forum

Some sites/businesses would not benefit from the inclusion of a forum. For example, if your product or service is not the type of product that will get talked about, then why add this facility? Also, as mentioned earlier, they can be open to abuse, both from disgruntled customers and competitors. It is not uncommon for competitors to disguise themselves as disgruntled customers and to post tales of woe after 'purchasing' your products!

Content is King

Flash: When to use it and when to not use it

You may also have heard of Flash or Shockwave, both Macromedia products. These are much more media-rich than standard graphics, allowing full animation, sound and interaction – there are even Flash games on the Internet. They also have another major benefit – they 'stream'! If a Flash 'movie' is 250kb, taking a minute or so to download via a standard modem, the image may start to play after only a couple of seconds. Then, while the rest of the image is loading in the background the Flash movie will continue playing. You might, for example use Flash to create an interactive tour of a product, which could also include narration and video. Mobile phone makers Sony Ericsson (www.sonyericsson.com) has used this to good effect when launching new models – users can see the phone interface on-screen and interact to get a feel for how the product works. Standard HTML does not offer this form of flexibility.

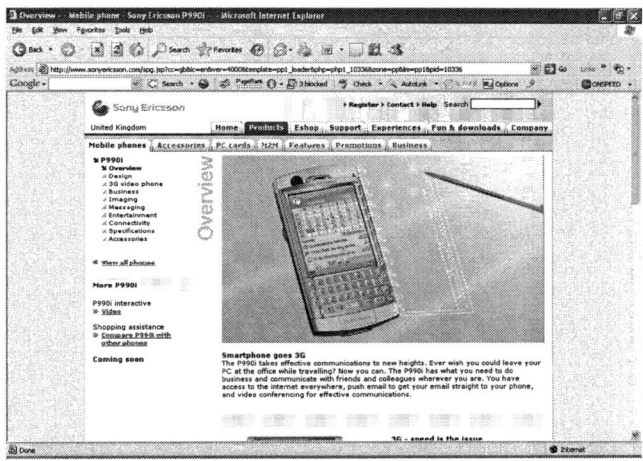

2.2. Flash can be used to good effect if used sparingly

There are some major drawbacks with Flash – most search engines cannot read inside a Flash file, so if your entire site is Flash-based then all most search engines will hit is a big brick wall! From a design point of view it is more time consuming to develop a Flash site than HTML, which of course generally equates to more expense. Therefore use Flash sparingly.

Don't steal content to bulk up on text
Search engines are known to compare pages across different sites, so if you

simply rip content from another site this can work against you. Also, ensure that you do not host duplicate pages on your site. The exact percentage of similarity after which a search engine may penalise you is not known, it varies from search engine to search engine, so your aim should be to keep your page similarity as LOW as possible.

Intro screens – No!

Do not succumb to the temptation of having an intro screen, which is usually either a static graphic or Flash animation that then leads into the main site. As mentioned above, if it's Flash then it'll stop search engines dead in their tracks. If it's a graphic then search engines can technically follow the link through to the rest of your content, but have little incentive to do so as there may be little or no text that it can 'see'.

What do search engines see, anyway?

Search engine databases are built by computer robot programs called spiders. Although it is said they 'crawl' the internet, they actually find pages for possible inclusion by following links in the pages they already have in their database (i.e. already 'know about'). They cannot just 'decide' to go look something up and see what's on the web about it, so if a web page is never linked to from any other page, search engine spiders cannot find it. The only way a brand new page – one that no other page has ever linked to – can get into a search engine is for its web address to be sent to the search engine companies as a request that the new page be included. How to do this is covered later in this book.

After spiders find pages, they pass them on for 'indexing'. This identifies the text, links, and other readable content on the page and stores it so that it can be searched. The page will be listed within a search engine's results page if your search matches its content.

If you want to get an idea of what a search engine will see when it hits your site use this free tool:

http://www.webconfs.com/search-engine-spider-simulator.php

This service will show you the raw text, URLs and keywords that search engines will see, without all of the graphics and formatting that your visitors will see – viewing your site in this rather undressed manner can give you a much better understanding of the task in hand.

Content is King

Spidered Text :
Marketing your Business - Martin Bailey - web consultancy, search engine optimisation, marketing assistance - Home Home MARKETING YOUR BUSINESS The official site for Martin Bailey and the book: Marketing your Business Tuesday, December 27 2005 Main Menu Home About the book/author About this site Consultancy Media Gallery Contact the Author Site Map Resources Web Resource Links Marketing tips Factsheets Product Reviews A bit of fun! Recommend this site Recommended items Domain search Glossary of Terms Online Store Categories Books (3) Software (4) Consultancy (1) Show Cart Your Cart is currently empty. Login Login below. Username Password Forgotten your password? No account yet? Create one Register to receive free marketing tips newsletter. 0) { mosLoadModules ("top"); echo "; }--> Welcome to Marketing your Business, by Martin Bailey Written by Martin Bailey Welcome to marketingyour.biz - the web site to accompany the new business marketing and promotion book from Martin Bailey. This site continues where the book leaves off and provides a continually updated resource of information and ideas.What's this site for/what's on the site:Buy the book 'Marketing your Business' onlineRequest a quote for web design/consultancyRead reviews of useful software and hardware productsRead/download marketing tips and tricksFind links to various web resources You can also register free on this site to receive our marketing newsletter, containing tips and advice.What's on the Marketing CD-ROM?To ensure that your business gets the most value from the book, the accompanying CD-ROM includes trial versions of many of the applications covered, such as Macromedia and Adobe products, together with several low-cost or even free products, including a complete 'Office' suite! There are now also several video tutorials included on the disc. [more...] Coming soon - New reviews of:Sony HDR-HC1E high definition camcorderGroupmail 5Adobe Creative Suite 2 Premium (CS2)Marketing your Business by Martin Bailey is available to buy from this website and all good retailers. Martin Bailey is available for consultancy, design and training services. Factsheet: Protecting your PC against viruses and spyware Written by Martin Bailey Spyware, trojans, dialers and viruses can cripple your PC's performance, destroy data and compromise your security. Find out how to identify if your PC is at risk and how to lock it down from attacks in the future by reading this factsheet. Read more... Press release: Martin Bailey signs up to write three new titles Written by Martin Bailey This is the official Press release announcing the signing of Martin Bailey to write three new titles for Management Books 2000 Ltd. The books will cover building a basic web site, using CMS systems and getting more visitors to your web site. Read more... [Back] Top of Page Latest Items Factsheet: Protecting your PC against viruses and spyware Review: Macromedia Studio 8 Press release: Second edition of Marketing your Business Press release: Martin Bailey signs up to write three new titles Review: Sony Ericsson K750i 2Mpixel phone Revenue Search Site Book Quotes '"Find the most motivating truths about your brand and communicate it to your most important consumers in the most single minded and bravest manner. They will respect you for it.'" - Kevin Dundas - Saatchi & Saatchi Polls What generates better leads? Printed Mailshots Email-shots Product reviews Web Enquiries Is your website written: In-house By a friend By a professional company Not at all (don't have one) © 2005 Martin Bailey - Marketing your Business

2.3. The marketingyour.biz website – as seen by search engines

Summary

Without content a site is just a skeleton - make sure that your site is well nourished with plenty of fresh pages. Later on we'll discuss how you can tweak the content so that users can find it easily, but for now just keep pumping out that text!

3. Finding the Right Keywords

This is the number one priority for anyone looking to optimise a site for search engines. You may think you know what words and phrases people are using to find sites similar to yours, but you will probably be quite surprised and shocked by the time you reach the end of this chapter!

The offline approach
Start by ensuring that you ask all new prospects how they found you. Even if they did not find you using a search engine ask them what they might have typed to find a company/product such as yours. Make a note of these for later. While you may disagree with some of the answers, you have to respect that these are genuine and that there may be others out there using the same words.

The online approach
There are several online tools that can help you to select the best words and phrases based on live search data. Of course Google has one such instrument – Sandbox. This free and extremely useful tool is hidden within their Adwords service, but you can access it directly at the following web address:

https://adwords.google.com/select/main?cmd=KeywordSandbox.

(If this is not working by the time you read this, do a Google search for 'Google Sandbox').

Getting More Visitors to Your Website in 90 Minutes

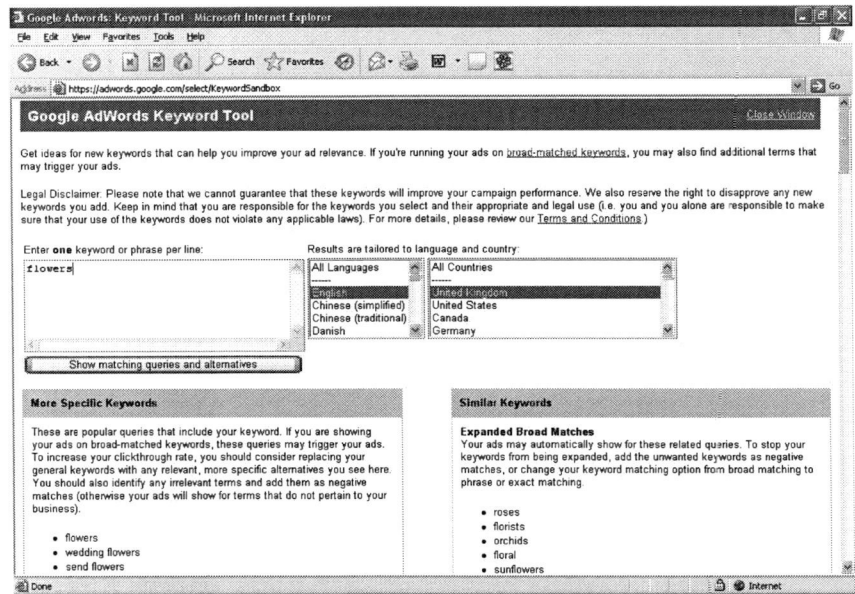

Fig 3.1 Google Sandbox can suggest alternative keywords based on real-world searches.

Start by entering either a keyword or phrase in the box, selecting the relevant language and country and then clicking the submit button. Google will check its databases and give you a list of specific and similar matches. It won't tell you which are the most popular phrases, but there are other ways to find this information out!

You can also try Google's 'AJAX-powered' Suggest, at http://www.google.com/webhp?complete=1&hl=en – this looks like the traditional Google search, but as you type each letter, it provides you with possible keywords, along with the number of results – this is useful for seeing the difference between single and plural keywords.

Overture provides a similar keyword search service at http://inventory.overture.com – entering a keyword will show you the frequency of searches for similar words or phrases for the previous month. This system is great for checking the popularity of terms that are currently in use. Note of course that the more popular a term, the stiffer the competition you'll face. You should use this on all of your terms to gauge their popularity, and then ensure that you optimise your site for the most important ones.

Finding the Right Keywords

If you want to take your keyword accuracy to another level, then it is worth considering Wordtracker (www.wordtracker.com). This is one of the most widely-used keyword assessment tools online today. Wordtracker works by compiling a database of terms that people search for. You enter keywords on their site and they'll provide you with in-depth analysis of those terms, including:

- how often people use the same words
- competing sites that use the same words
- keyword combinations that are relevant to your business
- your potential for gaining top 10 ranking in major search engines, broken down by search engine
- identify misspellings of keywords that may be worth optimising for.

All of this invaluable data does come at a price, although there is a free 15 keyword trial. Pricing is based on a subscription period, from one day to an annual fee.

When evaluating keywords or phrases you need to balance the popularity against the competition. Wordtracker helps you do this effectively by suggesting relevant alternatives and then showing you where they are used. In this way you can quickly identify the keywords where you are likely to face less competition.

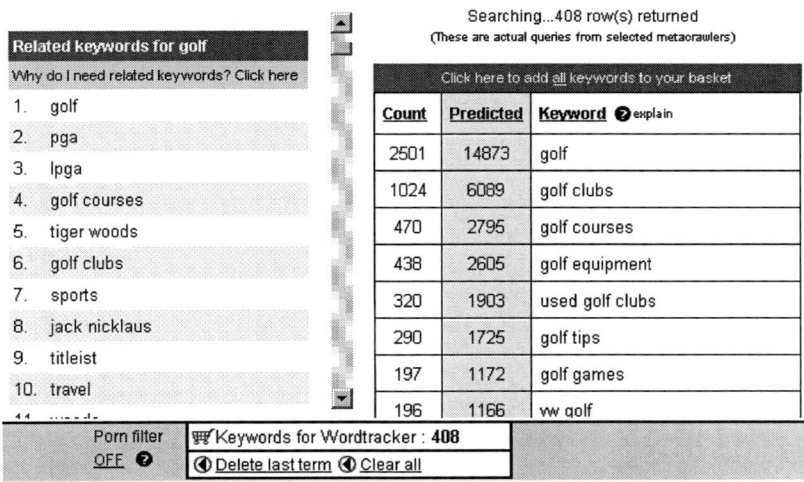

Fig 3.2. A search often yields a variety of possible words and phrases that you may not have considered.

As you dig deeper into the results, Wordtracker also appends a Keyword Effectiveness Index (KEI) number. This measures a keyword's competitive power and is a combination of the number of times it appears across the web against the breadth of sites that it appears on. The trick is to select words that obtain a high KEI rating across a lower number of sites. Use this in conjunction with other services such as Overture or Google Sandbox to find new keywords and rate their effectiveness.

There are also offline tools that help you analyse keywords on your sites and your competitors. Web CEO is one such tool, and there is a freeware version with a number of features relevant to several sections within this book – more on that later! Download the free version at www.webceo.com, install it and create a free account. Add a new site, go back to the front menu and select 'Research Keywords' and then select the site you just created. You can now either enter some keywords to research or load them from your site. WebCEO will then provide you with the number of daily searches done on your words, the number of competing sites and the KEI.

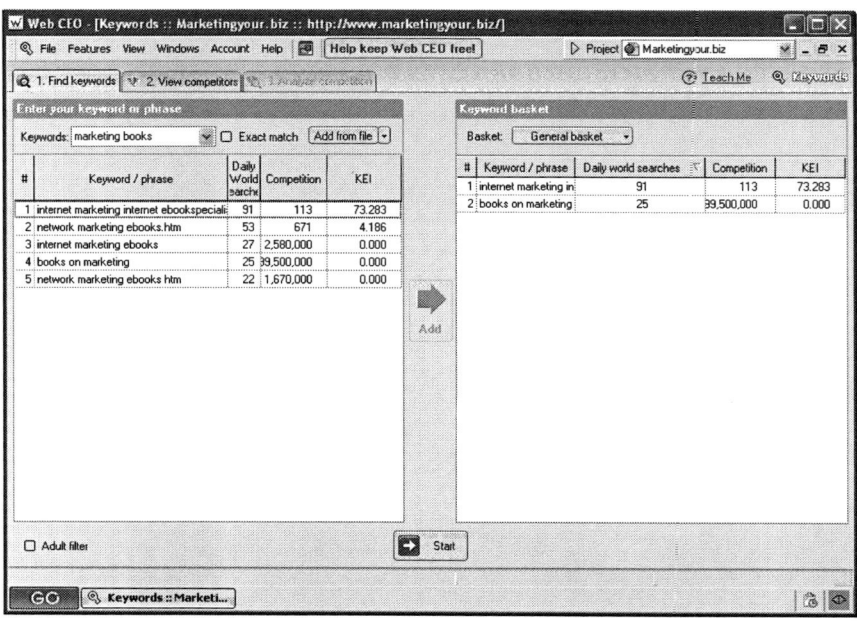

Fig 3.3 WebCEO can help you analyse the keywords on your site and your competitors'

Finding the Right Keywords

> **Summary**
>
> Choosing the right keywords is paramount, and forms the basis of everything you will do from here forward. Spend time to evaluate the keywords of your competitors and compile your list of 'must-use' keywords. Keep in mind that later you will optimise specific pages for specific keywords.

4. Adding Meta Tags to Your Site

This is the number one mistake that companies new to web promotion make – the omission of any Meta tags from their website. A Meta tag is a hidden piece of code that is there specifically to tell search engines about your site. Note that adding Meta tags alone is not a magic wand for your site's immediate number one placement, and less importance is placed upon them by search engines than in previous years, but they will assist some search engines in providing additional information about your pages.

Meta tags reside in the <HEAD> area of an HTML page. If you right-click over most web pages in your browser and select 'View Source' you will see that these pieces of code generally appear near the top of the page.

There are several different types of Meta tag that can be used, but we'll concentrate on the main ones for now:

Keywords:
This is where you list the words that users are most likely to use within search engines to locate your site. You created these words earlier on, so it's simply a case of putting these words into the code below. You can list up to around 1000 characters, with each word separated by a comma. Many search engines will only index the first 64 characters, so put the most important words first.

<meta name="keywords" content="keyword1, keyword2, keyword3, keyword4 ">

Description:
This is a paragraph that describes your company and/or site. It can be 200 characters in length, although some engines only display the first 20 characters, so ensure that these include the main item of interest (either company name, product name or product type). Include important keywords near the front of the description. Google does not use the Meta description in its listings; it automatically generates its own description instead.

<meta name="description" content="We sell tables, chairs and kitchen furniture. This is a short paragraph about our company and the products that we sell, with several keywords relevant to our

industry such as chairs, tables, kitchens.">

The following Meta tags are optional and are unlikely to affect rankings, although are still useful to include. Some search engines do not use them.

Company:
Some search engines will use this tag to categorise your site by company name

    <meta name="company" content="ABC Limited">

Homepage:
Where a site may span several servers and may even have several URLs this tag helps search engines identify where the home page resides.

    <meta name="homepage" content= "http://www.your_url_here.com">

Pragma:
This tag forces some search engines not to cache your content, thus ensuring users get to see the most up-to-date content.

    <meta http-equiv="pragma" content="no-cache">

Expires:
Ensures that search engines recognise that the content of your pages does not have a specific expiry date (as some sites do). If an expiry date were set and a search is performed after that date your page would not appear.

    <meta http-equiv="expires" content="0">

Distribution:
Only add this tag if your site is not limited to your own region or country. It specifies that the content on your site is for global distribution.

    <meta name="distribution" content="Global">

Rating:
Most sites are suitable for viewing by all ages, but where you have content that should not be viewed by minors you can specify this by changing the content to 'mature', 'restricted' or '14 years'. Parents can then enable the ratings system in their web browser (Tools, Internet Options and Content in Internet Explorer) to restrict access.

    <meta name="rating" content="General">

Adding Meta Tags to Your Site

Revisit-after:
The revisit-after meta tag is useful for sites where the content changes often and tells the search engine how often to revisit your site. The example below will tell the search engine to revisit your site every 7 days.

<meta name="revisit-after" content="7 days">

Robots:
This Meta tag is used to tell the search engine whether you want the web page indexed or not. You only really need to use this Meta tag if you DON'T want your web page indexed. The values for this tag are:

index(default)	Index the page
Noindex/index	Don't index the page/Index this page
Nofollow/follow	Don't index any pages hyper-linked to this page/Do index any pages hyper-linked to this page
None	Same as "noindex, nofollow"

<meta name="robots" content="follow, index">

Copyright:
This tag identifies the copyright owner of the page.

<meta name="copyright" content="ABC Limited">

Author:
Used to identify the author of the page.

<meta name="author" content="Author name">

Once you've completed your meta tags, the top of your page should look something like this:

<head>

<title>Your title here</title>

<meta name="description" content="ABC manufacture kitchen furniture such as tables, chairs, cabinets, shelves and complete fitted kitchen units.">

<meta name="keywords" content="kitchen, furniture, tables, chairs, units, shelves, abc">

<meta name="rating" content="general">

```
<meta name="copyright" content="ABC Limited">
<meta name="revisit-after" content="7 Days">
<meta name="expires" content="never">
<meta name="distribution" content="global">
<meta name="robots" content="index, follow'>
</head>
```

It is always good practice to move the Meta tags as near to the top of your HTML documents as possible. Some search engines only scan the first few kilobytes, so you want to make sure it's your Meta tags they are scanning.

Note: Do not add in competitor keywords into your Meta tags or you may find yourself at the wrong end of a lawsuit! Playboy Enterprises has successfully sued sites for using Playboy and Playmate in their Meta tags (and web addresses). It is not (yet) illegal to add in trademarked terms, however those that own the trademarks have the right to claim against you, and the stronger their brand the stronger the claim.

(If you find one of your competitors surreptitiously using your company or brand names within their Meta tags, or even hidden within the body of their pages you can report this to the search engine that you found them through. This will get them marked down or even blacklisted).

Adding Meta Tags to Your Site

Summary

Back in the 1990s, Meta tags were the holy grail of search engine submission, but search engines have got a lot wiser since then. They do still play a significant role in helping to correctly categorise your content, and some engines still use the description within their results listings, so while they do not hold the same level of importance you would be ill-advised to omit them.

5. Streamlining Your HTML Code – Stripping out the Dead Wood

Even when using the more advanced HTML editors, code can still get bloated. There are a number of tips and tricks that you can use however, to trim it down a little. Doing so not only makes your pages load faster, but makes them more search engine friendly. This is because search engines will 'weigh' keywords against the overall size of the document – this includes the code used to structure it, not just the content itself. Therefore where there is less code constructing the document more importance will be placed on your content.

Step 1 – Convert to CSS (Cascading Style Sheets)
In older versions of the HTML language tags such as <font>, <b> and <i> were used to specify the characteristics of text. Tables were (and for the most part still are) used to position text, menus and graphics. CSS has replaced the need to format content within the HTML page, allowing you to specify the look and feel of every element with much leaner commands held in an external file. It has also given a greater flexibility for other elements – for example you could change the size, colour and border of fields in a form, or create a simple 'hover' effect for a menu using CSS.

CSS can control the complete design style while the HTML code can contain the content. In practice most people use CSS to control little more than fonts and colours, which at least is a start! Even if your site is too complex or you do not have the knowledge/resources to fully convert it to CSS it is worthwhile to strip out some of the basic formatting to downsize your code.

An excellent place to better understand the concept of separating these elements is www.csszengarden.com. This site and accompanying book was created to demonstrate that CSS sites needn't be either complex or boring. A single HTML page was created containing only the content, and web designers around the world were allowed to submit different CSS designs that would apply layout and images to it. Essentially they created a CSS file and some graphics – the difference in the resulting sites is truly surprising! This is an excellent site for both inspiration and guidance on what CSS can do, and may persuade you that it's worth the pain to learn.

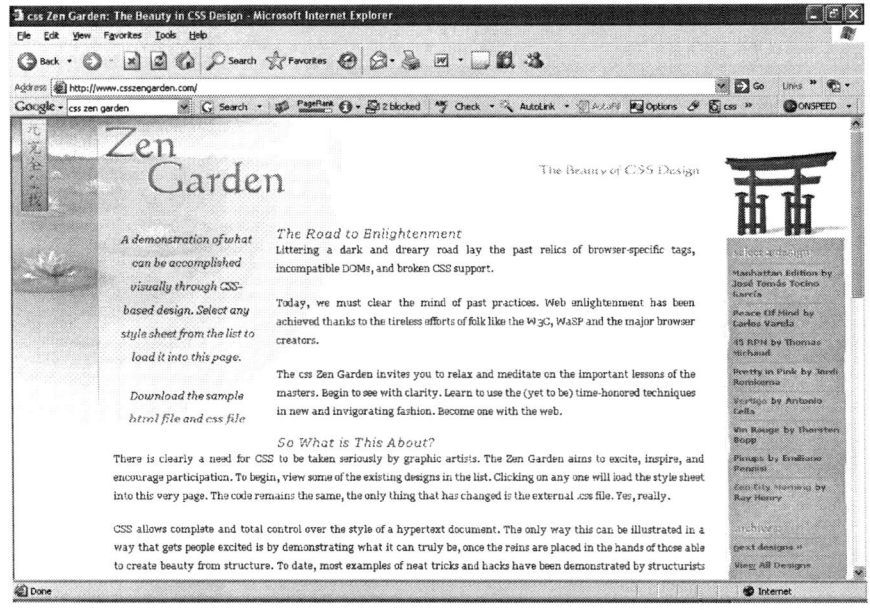

Fig 5.1. The CSS Zen Garden can bring inspiration and knowledge!

The culprit that generally bloats HTML code the most is the <font> tag. Imagine a page where every paragraph (or even every line has:

<font face="Arial, Helvetica, Verdana" size="2" color="#000000">

and then is finished with </font>...

With CSS, you can set the standard font, size, colour, spacing and much more with a single command, loaded once at the start of the document. Indeed, this can be applied site-wide! Once you create your Cascading Style Sheets they can be attached to any page, which means that updating the CSS file automatically updates the page. If you are using a template, generally the CSS file will be loaded within the 'locked' template area and will therefore appear across every page of your site. So you then have the ultimate flexibility of being able to change many elements of your site's look and feel by changing a few lines of code in a single file!

There are two ways that we can create CSS information. If you're using a template, you might want to start by creating it within the page, and then stripping it out as mentioned later in the chapter. Alternatively, if you have the knowledge you can create the CSS page from scratch.

For most sites you can start by creating a very basic CSS structure, covering:

- page title, background, border spacing (padding)
- font face, colour, size and placement
- hyperlink face, colour, size, mouse rollover effects
- heading font information.

Dreamweaver allows you to create this information very easily. Open up your template document and click Modify, then Page Properties.

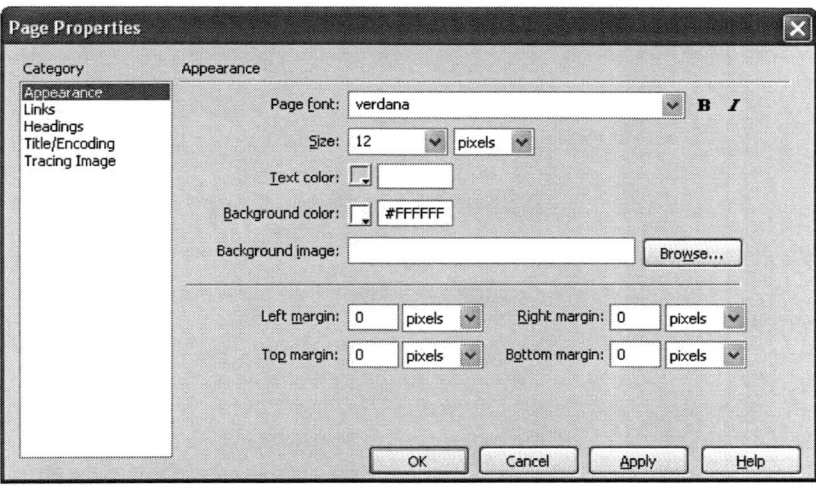

Fig 5.2: You can build a comprehensive CSS structure using this simple dialog window.

Under the appearance tab, you can specify the general font design, which will automatically apply to all text within the body, paragraph sections and tables (unless other styles are also applied to them). Next select Links and choose your colours and font style. Now click on Headings and change these accordingly. As soon as you click on OK, Dreamweaver inserts a whole ream of CSS data into the <HEAD> section of the page.

Getting More Visitors to Your Website in 90 Minutes

```
<!DOCTYPE html PUBLIC "-//W3C//DTD XHTML 1.0 Transitional//EN"
"http://www.w3.org/TR/xhtml1/DTD/xhtml1-transitional.dtd">
<html xmlns="http://www.w3.org/1999/xhtml">
<head>
<meta http-equiv="Content-Type" content="text/html; charset=iso-8859-1" />
<title>Untitled Document</title>
<style type="text/css">
<!--
body,td,th {font-family: Arial, Helvetica, sans-serif; font-size: 12px; color: #333333;}
body {background-color: #FFFFFF;}
a {font-family: Arial, Helvetica, sans-serif; color: #FF0000;}
a:link {text-decoration: none;}
a:visited {text-decoration: none; color: #FF0000;}
a:hover {text-decoration: underline; color: #0000FF;}
a:active {text-decoration: none; color: #FF0000;}
h1 {font-size: 18px; color: #000099;}
h2 {font-size: 16px; color: #000099;}
h3 {font-size: 14px; color: #000099;}
-->
</style></head>

<body>
</body>
</html>
```

Fig 5.3. Generating complex CSS code is easy with Dreamweaver

The above example would allow you to remove all font tags that control general font face and size, including those within headings, paragraphs and hyperlinks.

Even using CSS partially can still result in excessive code if you are not careful. Creating many different styles and then applying them throughout your site can mean that you apply multiple instances of a style when one instance in the right place would have done the same job. For example, if you have a table of 5 columns and 5 rows, and apply a font styling to each paragraph in each cell, that is 25 instances of *<P class="myclass">*, when you could have applied this style once when you create the table.

CSS does require a little time and experimentation to master, but the results are well worth it!

Step 2 – Strip out the CSS

Now we've put our CSS code in the top of our HTML page we want to take it out! The idea is that by stripping the CSS into a separate file and calling it from the HTML document it will be cached by the local web browser. If the same CSS file is used in conjunction with your template then that CSS file will load once with your first page, but will not need to reload as the visitor browses each subsequent page. This makes your site faster to load and

Streamlining Your HTML Code

reduces the amount of bandwidth you use – important for busy sites and for visitors on slower connections.

Creating a separate file is simple – just cut and paste everything inside (but not including) the <!-- and --> sections of the above code and save it in a separate file called styles.css (or whatever you want). Now amend the top line to be:

> <style type="text/css" src="styles.css"></style>

Note that you still need the end </style> tag, but this now appears immediately after the above tag, e.g. you're deleting everything including the <!-- and --> tags. If the styles.css file is not in the same directory as your HTML file or template ensure that this is reflected in the path.

Once you have your style sheets loaded you then have the arduous task of going through every document to locate the relevant formatting commands and removing them. There is a way to automate this, but use with caution! Dreamweaver has a 'tag remove' function – select Commands, Clean up HTML and enter the tag in Specific tags. Using this indiscriminately can cause all sorts of problems. If, for example you used the font tag to control the colour of a font, unless you specified this in the CSS the colour will be lost – not good if you created some table headers with black backgrounds and white text – the font will default back to black! So, while this is a quick way strip out superfluous tags it is also the quickest way to destroy your site if you are not careful!

Step 3 – Strip out the JavaScript

JavaScript code is used to perform functionality that HTML cannot, such as opening popup windows or adding intelligent features to forms. This same stripping technique can be applied to JavaScript code to further slim down your code.

An example of the sort of code you might have is as follows:

> <script language="JavaScript" type="text/JavaScript">
> <!--
> function MM_openBrWindow(theURL,winName,features) { //v2.0
>   window.open(theURL,winName,features);
> }
> //-->
> </script>

This is only a small piece of code, but invariably today's sites can have several times the amount of code, all of which has to load and be scanned before the search robot gets to your content – don't forget that some search engines only scan a few kilobytes of a page, so if the first 4kb is JavaScript you are seriously limiting the content they can get to. As with the style sheet we can replace this by making a separate file and calling it from the main document. Here's how to do it:

1. Locate the <script language="JavaScipt"> section from within the <HEAD> part of your page.
2. Start by selecting all of the text between (but excluding) <!-- and //--> tags
3. Cut it from the document (CTRL & C) to the clipboard, open Notepad, paste the text and save it with a .js extension e.g. script.js
4. Now modify your script as follows:

   <script language="JavaScript" src="script.js" type="text/javascript">

   </script>

Note: Ensure that the HTML page is located in the same directory as your script file, or change the path within src="" accordingly.

Summary

By moving the JavaScript and CSS out of your site, and optimising your code you can quite easily reduce a page's file size by 20%, all of which helps search engines get at the content they are interested in, as well as improving your visitors' experience of the site and reducing your bandwidth requirements.

6. Optimising Your Site for Your Keywords

Previously we discussed the importance of content and keywords. This is where we start to apply what we learnt! By now you should (hopefully) have a site that has a wealth of content, and an idea of the keywords that visitors are likely to use to find your site. The next step is to inject these keywords into the relevant places of your pages for optimum potency.

Remember that different pages will be optimised for different keywords. You probably have several different products or services – every page relating to each product needs to be optimised for keywords relating to that product. Keep this in mind as you go through and optimise each element of your page. Look at competing sites that rank highly and see what methods they have employed.

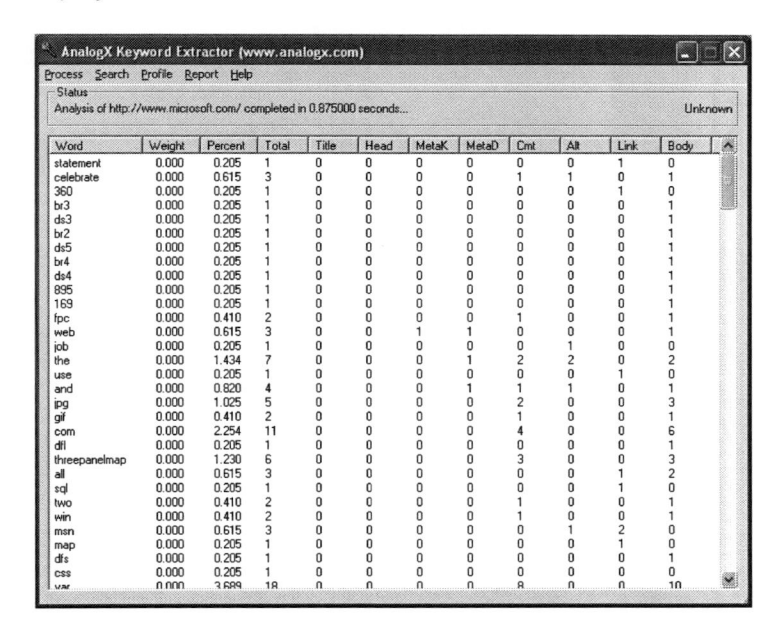

6.1 Analog Keyword Extractor can help you get an idea of what keywords to use and where to place them

An excellent free tool you can use is the Analog Keyword Extractor. This basic but functional application allows you to enter a URL and then see a breakdown of keywords and where they are placed within each HTML element of the page. Again, run some competing URLs through the keyword extractor to see which words they are optimising for and the weight placed upon them. If you just want a quick tool to show you keyword weight, sorted by density then this fits the bill nicely.

We mentioned WebCEO in chapter 3, which also provides much more detailed analysis of your chosen keywords and their placement. While Analog Keyword Extractor gives you a 'quick hit' of keywords WebCEO will literally tell you where you are going wrong. This is covered in detail further on in the chapter.

File names
Before we even look at the keywords within your text you should consider the name that you give to every page. Rather than 'prod1.htm' use a keyword within the page name. Separate words with a hyphen instead of spaces as files with spaces (or indeed capitals) can cause problems on UNIX web servers. Keep filenames down to a sensible length (2-3 words).

Page title
This is BY FAR the most important element of your page for keyword optimisation. Not only should keywords appear in the title, but they should also appear nearer the front of the title. The page title is the text that appears in the blue taskbar at the top of the screen, and is controlled by the <TITLE> tag within the <HEAD> section of your page. Do not make the age-old mistake of just having your company name in the title – who is going to search for that? On your index page ensure that your main product, service or industry is covered in the first two or three words of the title. Now go through every page on your site and ensure that the page title uses the most potent keywords based on your initial research.

Titles (H1, H2, H3 etc)
In addition to the page title containing keywords, the actual title that describes the main content is also critical, as search engines place more importance on text placed within title tags. Text should be contained within <H1> tags, and of course (e.g. <H1>Golf Clubs</H1>). By default H1 text will be huge, so create a new style within your CSS file to make this match your site. This could be along the lines of:

H1 {font-size=14px;}

Optimising your Site for Your Keywords

It is good practice to set styles for H1-H6 tags, and then use them to distinguish subtitles within your pages. Ensure that keywords that appeared in the page title (<TITLE> tag) also appear in your H tags. In many cases, the page title and the H1 title could be identical.

Page content
With any luck, much of your content will already contain the keywords you have harvested, but their placement within the page can make all the difference. In addition to keywords appearing in the page title and header tags they should also appear near the top and bottom of your page, in the first and last paragraph. They should also be spread liberally throughout the content.

As a rule of thumb, pages should have at least 300 words, with main keywords having a weight of between 3-6%.

Hyperlink text
So our main text is now in good shape, but what about links in and out of each page? Instead of having 'click here' as the text within a hyperlink to a page (or, worst still, all graphics which search engines cannot read), add in keywords to the hyperlink text e.g. See more golf clubs here. If you've followed the instructions so far, you'll have pages with keywords in the filename, page title, header title, content and now with other pages linking to them with the same keywords.

ALT text
Most of your pages will contain images. While search engines cannot (yet) read text within images you can add 'alternative' text that they can. This text delivers several benefits:

- If users have disabled graphics from loading (perhaps because they are on a slow connection) then the ALT text will show up in place of the image
- ALT tags are actually required for your site to be compliant with the latest web standards
- As ever, ALT tags with relevant keywords add further weight to the overall importance of the page

Adding ALT tags is simple, whichever software you are using. Within Dreamweaver, just click on the image, and enter the relevant text within the Alt field

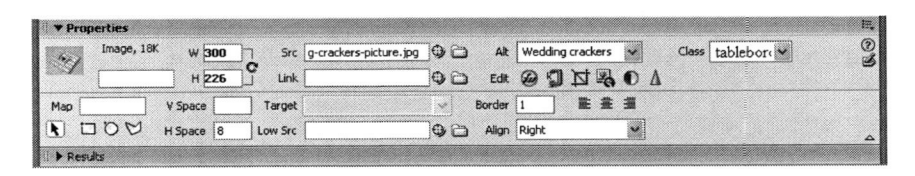

6.2. Adding ALT tags to an image is simple in Dreamweaver

You can also easily add ALT tags in using a HTML source code editor. Just locate the <IMG> tags within the code and add in ALT='Your text here' anywhere within the <> characters. So a completed tag might look like:

<img src="/images/pic.gif" alt="A line containing keywords">

It is important to do this for every image on your site. If there are images that do not warrant alternative text – an example being a small corner graphic – you can just add alt="".

Hyperlink 'title' text

This trick is not actually used as much as it could be on many sites. You can add the equivalent of an ALT tag to a hyperlink, which provides the same tooltip information rectangle when the mouse is hovered over a text link as the ALT text described above. And as with the ALT tag, it's just as easy to achieve – just add TITLE="Your description of the hyperlink here". A completed tag might be:

<a href="pagename.htm" title= "A description of the hyperlink here which includes keywords relevant to the page you are linking to."

In addition to making your site more user-friendly and more accessible, it yet again increases the overall weight of those all-important keywords within your total page.

Buying additional domain names

Even if you already have what you regard as a good domain name, e.g. your company name, from a search engine point of view it may not be winning you brownie points. You can actually have more than one domain name pointing at the same site, although you must ensure you use the right method to point it. Let's say you have 'yourname.com' and also buy 'yourproduct.com', which you want to point at the main site. The easiest method is to have a single page that actually has no real content; instead it has a piece of code that immediately forwards the user to the 'real site'. (For the more technical amongst you, it is a meta tag with a refresh command set

Optimising your Site for Your Keywords

to 0 seconds and the forwarding URL of your 'real' web address). This is NOT the way to do it! The second method, also similarly despised by search engines, is to use frames. This is where your second domain opens up two pages – one that is usually 0 pixels high and the second calls the main site externally – this essentially masks the second domain in the address bar. Both methods are frowned upon and can confuse search engines, so the best way is to 'hard code' domains to the IP address rather than just forwarding it to another URL. This can be a problem with more basic hosting packages, so talk to your ISP about how they can lock several domains to your web space.

Buying an optimised domain name
Search engines also place importance on keywords appearing in the domain name itself, so it is worthwhile to purchase a domain with your top-most keyword(s) included in it. Of course, this is easier said than done, with most top level domains (.com) already taken. Identify your top key phrase and see if you can buy it, separating each word with a hyphen e.g. lightweight-golf-clubs.com.

One trick that can work quite well is to create an 'A NAME' record for your domain, creating a 'sub-domain'. You may have seen some sites that have something in place of the www part of their domain – it is relatively easy (with most ISPs) to create another record for the domain that points to the same place, such as golf-clubs.yourdomain.com. There are several benefits to this method.

- If you've owned the main domain for some time, search engines place more importance on older domains, so you are more likely to get a higher ranking than by buying a new domain with your keywords in.
- It's cheaper than buying a new domain.
- You can usually do this yourself through your ISP's back end control panel.
- Changes normally take effect within 24-48 hours.
- You can have dozens of A NAME records, and each of these could point at different locations if you desire.

Adding an A NAME record differs from ISP to ISP, so consult any online documentation for further information on how to do this. It normally involves logging into your domain control panel, editing the 'zone file' for your domain, creating a new line with your requested A NAME record (e.g. my-keyword.mydomain.com.) and the IP address (which will be the same as your main IP address.

Note that some shared hosting packages do not allow you to perform A NAME changes, so you may have to upgrade or change your host.

How to buy a domain name

Buying a domain is actually pretty simple. There are hundreds of ISPs in the UK alone that sell domains, and once you've found the ideal name the buying process is virtually the same as buying a book from Amazon. On the front page there will usually be a search field with 'Choose a domain' (or similar) close by. Enter your ideas for a domain name, adding the domain suffix (.co.uk, .com, .biz etc) afterwards. The search results page will tell you if it is available to buy. If it is free then it is simply a case of following the standard shopping cart process.

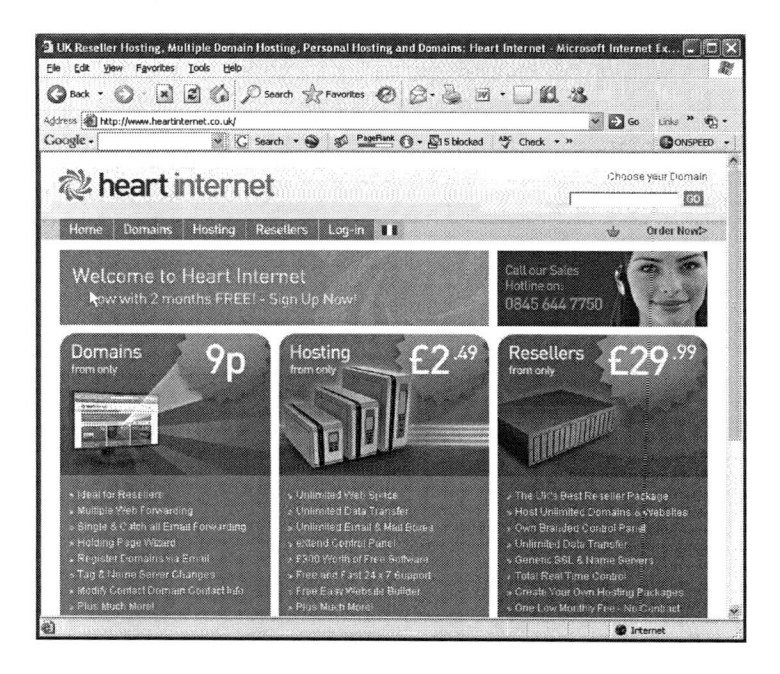

6.3 ISPs such as Heart Internet make it easy to buy multiple domains and point them at one address

Checking your optimisation

Once you've completely optimised your site you can use various tools to

Optimising your Site for Your Keywords

check your success. We mentioned WebCEO earlier, and now we are interested in its 'Optimise pages' facility. Open the software and add a site to the database and click on Optimise pages. Select your domain from the list and on the following page enter your keywords or let WebCEO download them from your site. You can also select an alternative page – if no other page is selected then your homepage will be used. Within a few seconds of clicking the start button you will be presented with an in-depth report of the quality of the page. Not only does it take your keywords into consideration but also the general quality of your HTML, so this will help you identify other problems with your code.

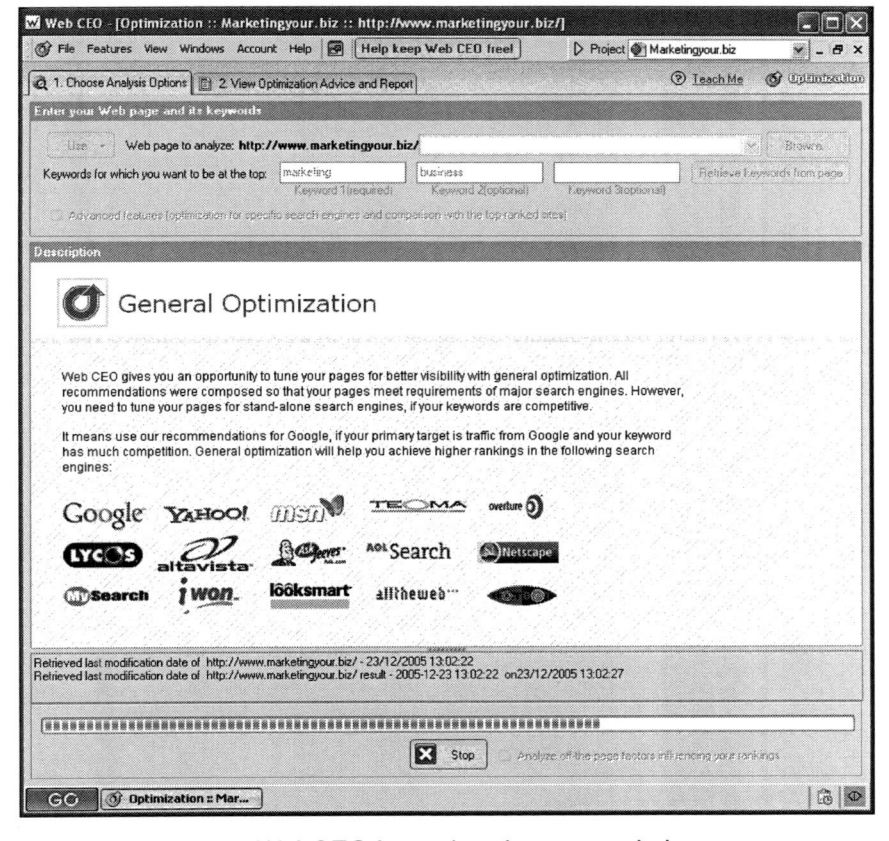

6.4. WebCEO has a handy page optimiser

Summary

After your site, content keywords are the most important (and often most overlooked) element of search engine optimisation. Optimise specific pages for specific keywords so that users employing more targeted keyword searches will get to your pages first. Buying domains with keywords in can add extra weight to specific searches. Use tools such as WebCEO to check the quality of your chosen keywords.

7. Building Site Maps

A site map is a page on your site that acts like a cross between a table of content and an index in a book – it gives both users and search engines a single point of reference to get to all the major sections and sub-sections within your website. All but the smallest of sites should have a site map – any site over 5-10 pages should have one.

What should a site map contain?
The site map is there to give visitors an understanding of how content is structured within your site. Site maps generally take the form of bulleted 'tree' navigation, so all of the top levels (e.g. home, products, technical etc) will be furthest to the left, with sub-levels indented to the right. The deeper within the site the content resides, the further to the right it will be indented. You do not necessarily have to link to every single page, but you should link to all main and sub levels. Remember the three click rule – users should be able to access any page within three clicks of the home page. If they can do that (quicker) by using the site map, then it has achieved its goal.

Why have a site map?
The first reason is answered above – it makes it easier for your visitors to find their way around. The second (and more important reason to my mind) is for search engine optimisation. A site map generally has the title of the page as the link text. If you have already optimised your title text with relevant keywords, then you will be using the very same text as your site map link description. Amongst other criteria a search engine ranks a page's importance on its content, page title (in blue bar at top of page), the title within the heading (<H1>) tags and pages *that link to it with the same keywords*. For example, if you have a page relating to kitchen bar stools, then 'kitchen bar stools' would appear in the title of the page, body content and also within the text of the hyperlink on your site map page. So a site map can help you to complete the criteria for a well-ranked page on a specific topic.

Creating a site map
How you add a site map to your site will very much depend on how your site is written. If it is built in static HTML and based around a template, then it is simply a case of creating a blank page based on your template, creating a

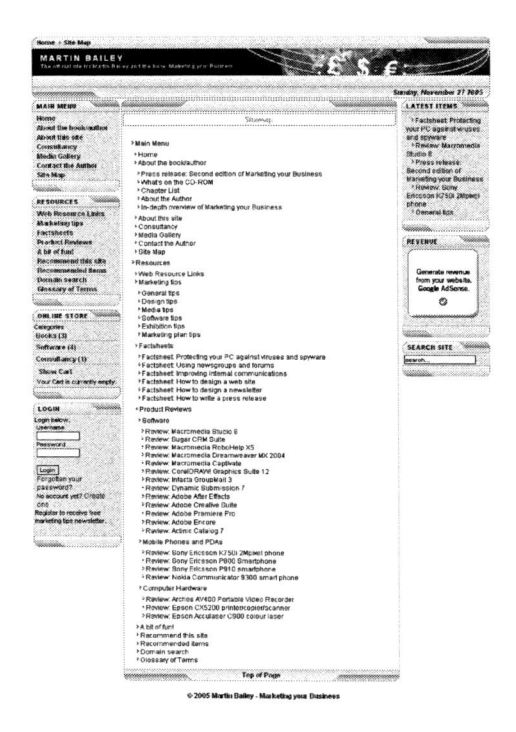

Fig 7.1 The marketingyour.biz site map

bulleted list of all of your main sections, and then adding in sub-sections and/or pages. Then you need to place a hyperlink to each page in turn. Even for a site with 100 pages this should only take 1-2 hours to complete, and is well worth the effort!

If you are using a Content Management System (CMS) such as Mambo, Joomla! or PHP-Nuke, there are generally site map components that will automate the process for you. The installation process will vary depending on the CMS system employed. Once installed, every time you add a new page or section it will automatically appear in your site map page without you having to lift a finger!

For dynamic sites that have been built in-house you can either build a static HTML page as described above or write a script to automate the process, however this may present you with some problems. The URL for dynamic pages may change, depending on how your site is built, so you won't be able to place static links to these pages. Building a dynamic method of populating a site map may present its own problems, and this will differ from site to site. Consult the author(s) of your site for more information.

Google site map
In 2005, Google opened yet another beta project – Google Site Maps. Google cite it as a 'collaborative crawling system allowing you to communicate with Google to keep it informed of changes to your site'. In other words you create a file that is not visible to visitors but that Google can see – this file contains a more detailed site map than a standard one that would appear on your site, detailing new pages and updates to old pages – and all of this is prepared to Google's preferred format. This is especially useful for dynamic sites that Google may have difficulty in spidering. As the web become more dynamic with the likes of AJAX, there may be no obvious way for a spider to discover some content on its own.

But that's not all! In line with Google's 'do no evil' mantra, they give you something back for providing them with your site information in their preferred format – information. In the tabbed site overview screen you can view information such as:

- top search keywords used and top keyword clicks
- status of pages crawled with a split of their PageRank status
- analysis of content type
- how the site is indexed (e.g. who links to it, who refers to it, similar pages etc).

Creating the XML formatted file that Google requires is not something you would want to undertake manually, even for the smallest of sites, but fortunately there are plenty of free tools out there to do the job for you. It is also possible to completely automate the process, so once done you never need worry about it again.

```
-<urlset>
 -<url>
    <loc>http://www.google.com/BUILD</loc>
    <lastmod>2005-04-30T03:45:08+00:00</lastmod>
  </url>
 -<url>
    <loc>http://www.google.com/about.html</loc>
    <lastmod>2005-05-07T00:45:09+00:00</lastmod>
  </url>
 -<url>
    <loc>http://www.google.com/addurl.html</loc>
    <lastmod>2005-03-11T23:45:16+00:00</lastmod>
```

Fig 7.2. The Google site map code can look a little frightening to the uninitiated!

Creating a Google Sitemap

There are several stages to creating the XML file that Google needs.

1. You need to register at www.google.co.uk/webmasters/sitemaps/ – this is free and if you have a Gmail account you can use that address. You can add as many domains to this account as you want. Once you've registered with Google, you will have immediate access to basic information, all of which is actually already available if you know Google's search bar syntax. For example – type site:www.yourdomain.com will show all pages indexed.

2. Next, use one of the many free Google sitemap creation programs to create the file for you – a quick 'Google' will provide hundreds of tools, but some good free ones can be found at www.auditmypc.com, www.xml-sitemaps.com, www.vigos.com and www.sitemapspal.com. Some process your pages online and others are downloadable applications that you install on your PC. Once you've run the generation process you'll end up with either an XML or plain format file, which may also be 'GZIPped' depending on the method you use. (GZIP is a file compression method, which can be useful if you have a large site that will generate a large sitemap file.)

3. Once you have your sitemap file, simply upload it to your web server. It must be placed in the root directory.

4. Now go back to Google, log in and from within the Site Overview section click on Add a sitemap. Select the type of sitemap (usually General web) and then click Next. On the next screen put in the exact URL to the

sitemap file that Google will need to access it e.g. http://www.yourdomain.com/sitemap.xml

Within 24 hours, Google will download and check the file. When you log back in you should see that there is now one sitemap associated with your domain. There is one more stage you need to complete in order to access the goodies that Google will provide you with – you need to verify the site. This is purely a security measure on Google's part, and is simply a case of creating a file with a name that Google provides you with, and then uploading the file to your root directory – click on Verify once done and Google then knows that you are the webmaster with access to the webspace.

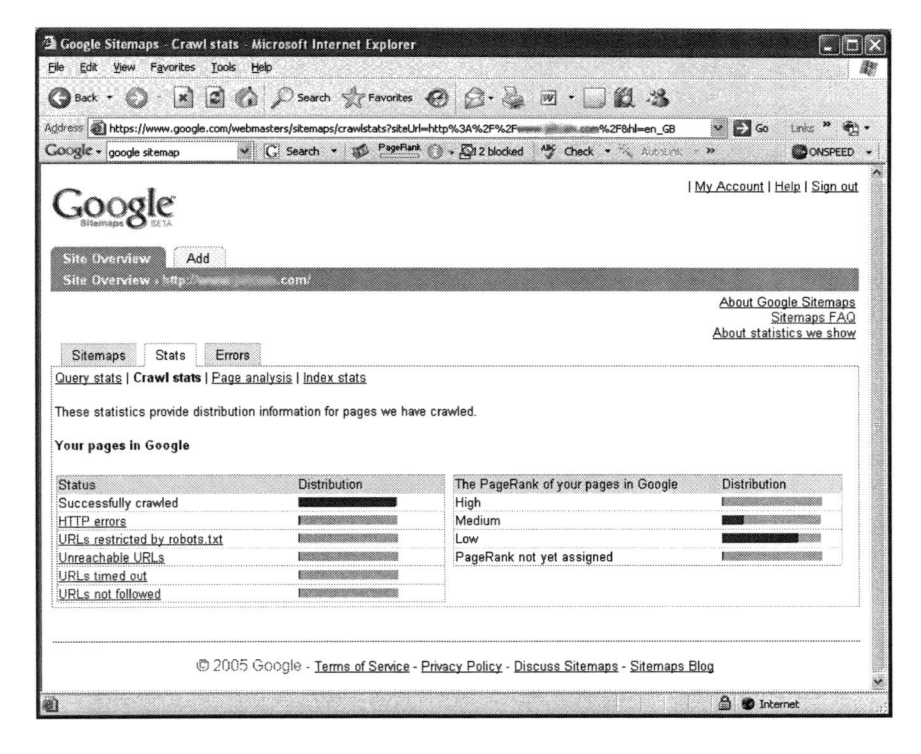

7.3. Once your site is verified Google will provide you with free information

So, whether you build a site map for visitors to use or create a Google Sitemap, you are providing an easy way for your content to be located and harvested.

> **Summary**
>
> A site map not only provides users with an easy way to navigate your content structure, but also gives search engines a surefire route around your site. You do not need to link to every single page – just the main pages and categories. Content Management Systems such as Joomla! or Mambo can automatically generate standard and Google site maps using free extensions.

8. Validating Your Web Code

It's all very well optimising your site with your chosen keywords, getting dozens of quality links back into it and submitting it to all of the search engines, but if the fundamental structure of the site is based on poor code, this will do you more harm than good. Web browsers can be both forgiving and frustrating in the way they will display sites. For example, go back a few years and ask any web designer about Internet Explorer versus Netscape Navigator. They will tell you horror stories of how they built sites that were beautiful in IE but that looked ghastly (or even failed to load altogether) in Netscape. The war of the browsers still rages on, with Opera and Firefox gaining ground on IE.

What is compliancy anyway?
The W3C (World Wide Web Consortium) set up web standards for the various different languages used to construct the web, including HTML, XHTML and CSS, along with accessibility standards. While you won't get fined if you break their rules, what you will have is a site that may not display correctly in different browsers, or be difficult to use for those with disabilities. Clean, valid code is generally less bloated, is easier to update and opens your site up to a wider audience who will appreciate the efforts you have gone through to make your site a friendlier place for them.

HTML vs XHTML
Regardless of whether you decide to use HTML or XHTML to write your pages, this will not change the way they appear to visitors. It is advisable to use the newer standard – XHTML (eXtensible HyperText Markup Language). Macromedia Dreamweaver can write XHTML without you even noticing, so it is advisable to leave the default setting of creating XHTML pages. This will allow additional functionality to be added much easier later on without having to rework all of your pages. As XHTML is much stricter than HTML, getting into the habit of writing compliant XHTML code may require a little more effort, but the stability and cross-browser compatibility is well worth it. It is not within the scope of this book to go into the differences and benefits of XHTML, so visit www.w3.org for further information. There are also some excellent free tutorials at www.w3schools.com. If you want to convert your site from HTML to XHTML there is a free validator at http://validator.aborla.net/ that not only points out the errors but also provides you with repaired code.

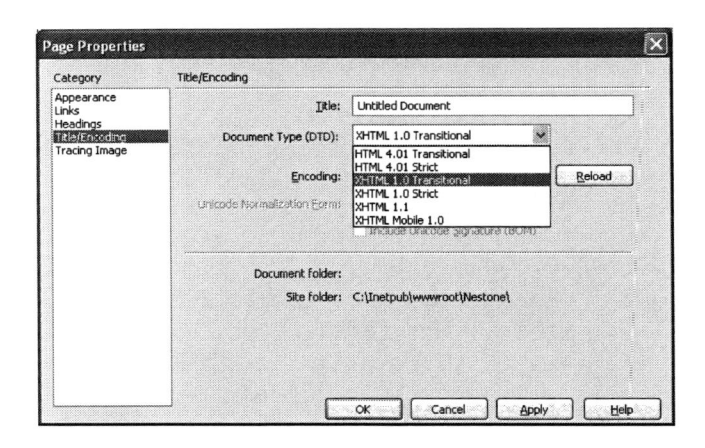

8.1. Specifying the right encoding type within Dreamweaver

Common errors

The most common errors in web code are tags that are not closed, or that are closed improperly. For example, you can start a paragraph of text with <p> and should close it with </p> – many programmers don't bother doing this as browsers will assume the paragraph is closed when it reads the next instruction within the code, but this will result in the page not being compliant.

Nesting tags incorrectly is another common mistake. When you open an HTML tag, the next instruction (unless it is a self-closing tag such as <IMG>) is a closing tag, e.g. This is bold. So while this is correct:

Bold and italic text

This is not:

Bold and italic text

Again, most browsers are quite forgiving and will display this correctly, but it is incorrect nevertheless and should be fixed.

Dead links are another cardinal sin of web design. As sites grow they can become unwieldy dinosaurs of content – this is especially true of very old sites that are not based on a template and do not employ any of the newer web standards such as CSS. If a page is linked to from several places, and that page is subsequently deleted it is easy for dead links to be buried deep within your site.

Validating Your Web Code

Tables, especially in complex structures can cause all manner of problems. Not closing a <tr> or <td> tag can cause some very strange effects in some browsers but appear normal in others. One site I worked on displayed correctly in IE but was about eight screens wide in Netscape Navigator because of a single missing code.

Where a site has been developed through cutting and pasting from MS Word (or, worst still, written in Word itself) the code can become horrendously bloated. Word adds style tags to almost every tag, and can easily double the size of a web page. While the code itself may be valid, it will cause errors when trying to apply a style sheet to a page, as the styles within the HTML page will override those from the CSS file.

Checking for errors

If you are using one of the more recent web development tools such as Macromedia Dreamweaver or Adobe GoLive you will have access to comprehensive validation tools.

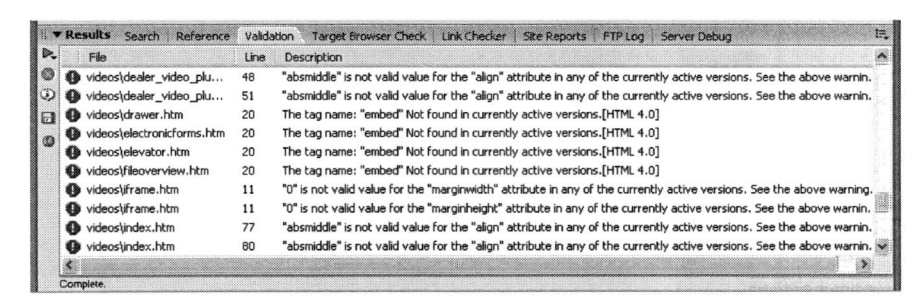

8.2. Dreamweaver can provide excellent code validation information.

Within Dreamweaver, press F7 to display the Results panel and select Validation. Click the Play icon to the left and select whether you want to validate a page or complete site. You can also select which standards you wish to validate for, which will depend on which code standard you have used to write your site. Normally you can leave this to the default setting, as this will be detected by Dreamweaver when the page opens. In the result table you will see a description of each error, along with the page filename and line number on which it occurred. Double-clicking on the filename will open the page in code view at the appropriate place so that you can amend the code. Once done save your page and revalidate to confirm that it is now compliant.

There is a small minority of items that simply will not validate, even though they display correctly in the browser, with the main culprit being embedded Flash items. These use the <embed> tag, which is no longer officially supported by current HTML standards. There is a dirty fix for this – turning the code that calls the Flash file into a JavaScript document (by using the document.write command), saving it as a separate file and then loading it using the <script> tag. This is for purists only, as the validation failure of this item alone will have no influence on your page rankings or your visitor's ability to view your page correctly.

Dreamweaver also provides a link validator and target browser checking facility within the same panel, providing a single location for identifying and fixing a variety of common issues. The procedure for running both of these is the same as general validation

One of the more useful tools within Dreamweaver is the 'Clean up HTML' facility. This handy function strips out empty and redundant tags, and will even combine font tags (although of course you will want to replace this with CSS code!). It can also strip out some MS Word formatting commands.

Valid code – what next?
If you've followed the above then you should have a site that has no dead links, has lean code and has no reported error. It should also work with all of the main browsers. But the validation is not yet complete! In my own tests, I have found that while Dreamweaver picks up the majority of validation issues it does not pick up all of them. Therefore the next step is to use the official validation tools, all of which are free.

W3C has two tools that offer a quick way to locate problems within HTML and CSS files, and also provides plenty of advice and information on how to solve them. To start with go to http://validator.w3.org and enter your URL. The results page will either display a congratulatory message that your code is compliant or list the errors, line numbers and description of any problems.

Validating Your Web Code

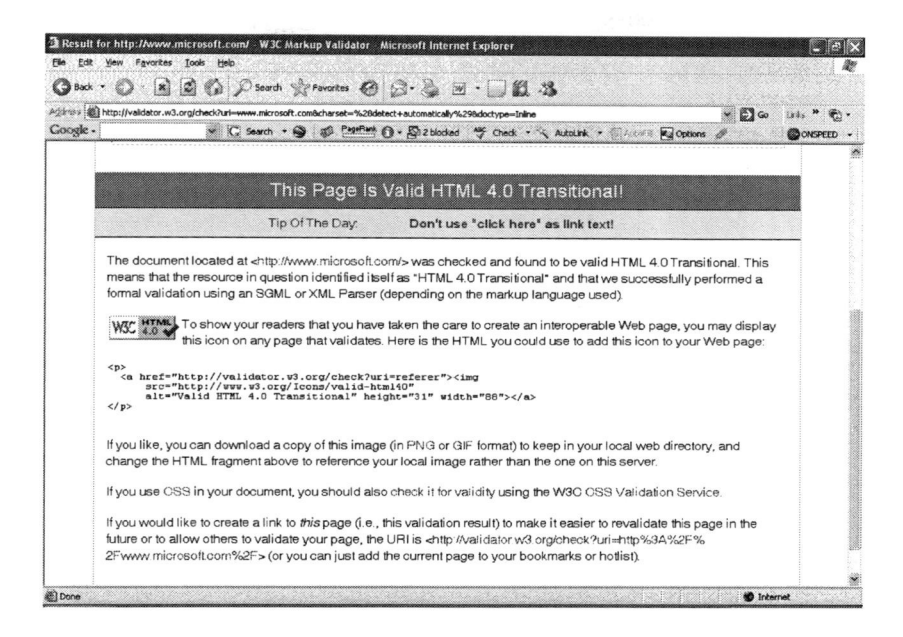

8.3. The much sought after W3C valid code page

Now that your HTML is valid you must also validate your CSS. This is a similar procedure – visit http://jigsaw.w3.org/css-validator/, enter your URL or a direct link to your CSS file and view the results on the following page. Even if your code validates, you will generally see a list of warnings and suggestions underneath which are worthwhile paying attention to. These normally apply to potential omissions rather than actual errors with your code. A common example is if no background colour has been applied to a style – the validator is effectively telling you that you might have dark text on a dark background simply because you have not specified that the background might be light.

I would place greater importance on trying to achieve validation of your CSS than HTML. CSS is much less forgiving than HTML, and a single error in a style can drastically change the appearance of a site. If you've converted your site to rely on CSS at least for font styles, and have removed all major errors and dead links within your HTML, then you have achieved more than most site designers, and will have a much leaner site that both search engines and users will benefit from.

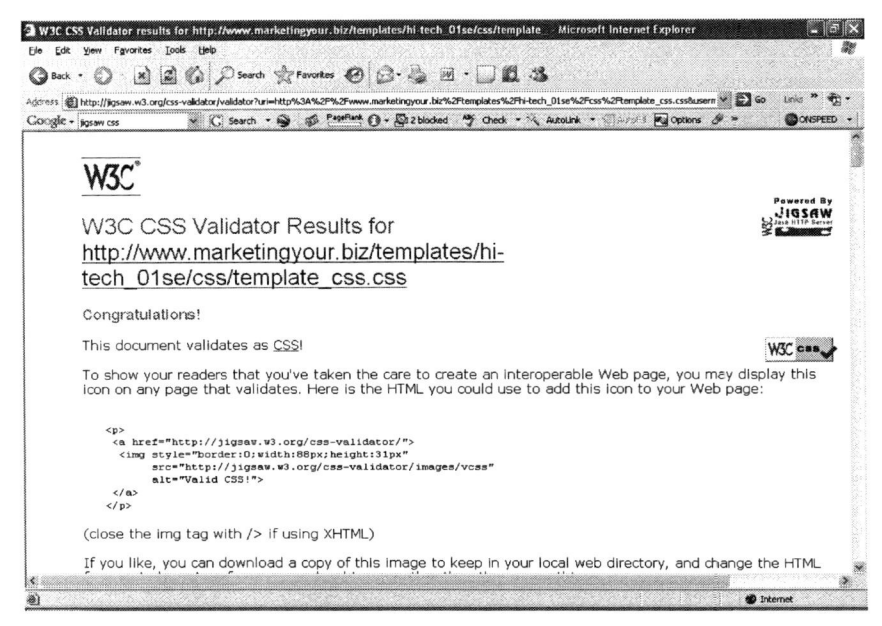

8.4. Validating CSS is even more important than validating HTML

Validation and content management systems
If you are using a CMS system such as Mambo, Joomla! or PHP-Nuke then it is difficult (and in some cases impossible) to get the site to validate 100%, and you will have to dig quite deep to fix most errors. The problems generally fall into two categories.

- **URL problems** – CMS systems generate complex URLs with characters and variables that are not compliant. Fortunately most CMS systems offer a 'SEO friendly' (search engine optimisation) option, which replaces these unwieldy addresses with something that not only validates but is easier for search engines to spider. The URL may not be optimised for keywords.

- **Template problems** – you have more than likely installed one of the many different templates available for your CMS. Many are written with great attention to code validity, but some are less carefully constructed. Therefore you will need to edit the template file(s) to make them compliant. This can be quite tricky, especially as many people choose a CMS specifically as they do not possess strong HTML experience. You are likely to be able to remove most of the problems from templates by doing this.

Validating Your Web Code

Checking for accessibility

Even though you have perhaps removed all errors from your HTML and CSS code, there is still one area that you should pay attention to – accessibility. Many countries are now bringing in new laws that require you to offer assistance to your visitors in the same way that a shop might have to provide wheelchair access. Millions of people have disabilities that affect their use of the Web. Currently most web sites have accessibility barriers that make it difficult or impossible for many people with disabilities to use the Web. As more accessible web sites and software become available, people with disabilities are able to use and contribute to the web more effectively.

Web accessibility also benefits people without disabilities. For example, a key principle of web accessibility is designing web sites and software that are flexible to meet different user needs, preferences and situations. This flexibility also benefits people without disabilities in certain situations, such as people using a slow Internet connection, people with 'temporary disabilities' such as a broken arm, and people with changing abilities due to ageing. To read more about the Web Accessibility Initiative (WAI) visit *www.w3.org/WAI/*.

You can check your site for accessibility by using a free online validator at http://webxact.watchfire.com/, which will break down the results into quality, accessibility and privacy sections. Accessibility results are further broken down into 'priority 1, 2 and 3', signifying the three levels of accessibility you can code for, with 3 being the best.

If you've employed all of the advice recommended so far, chances are that your site will immediately comply with priority 1, or require very little modification to make it compliant.

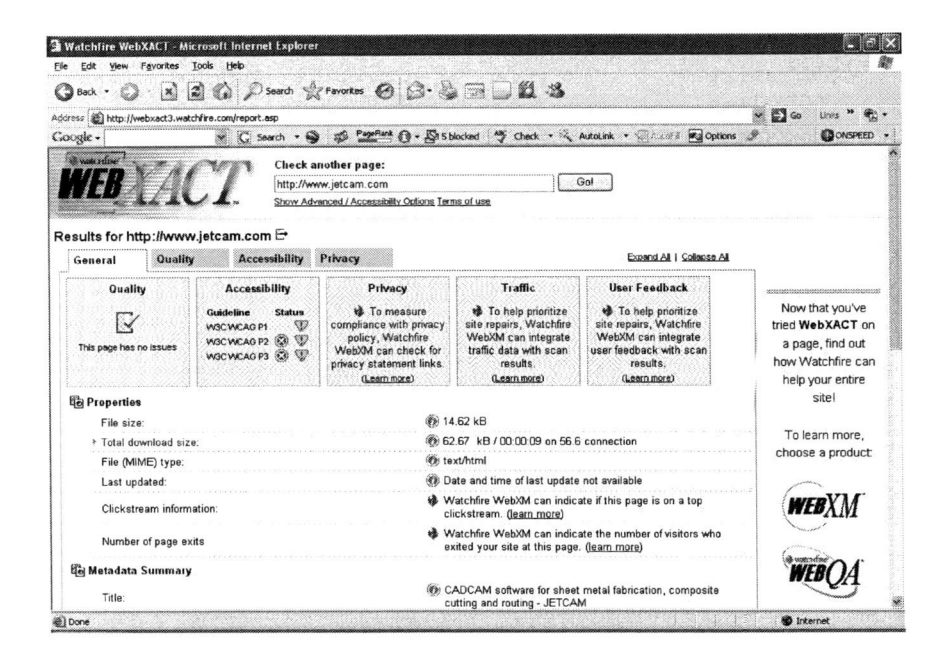

8.5. The WebXact site offers a free accessibility check for your site, and offers advice on how to fix problems

Test, test and retest

Even though you have tested your site against web standards some browsers may still not display it as intended. I have written totally compliant sites that display slightly differently in Firefox than in Internet Explorer. You should test your site in all of the main Windows browsers, which are:

- Internet Explorer (present and most recent version)
- Mozilla Firefox
- Netscape Navigator
- Opera

In addition to testing for the PC you should also test on Apple Macintosh browsers.

Finally, test at different screen resolutions. Most people use at least a screen size of 800 x 600, with 1024 x768 fast becoming the norm, so it's safe to design a site to one of these widths, but be aware of how it will look at lower resolutions.

Validating Your Web Code

Summary

While it may seem like a lot of effort to go through to check a site that looks OK when you browse it, remember that your visitors will be viewing it on different speed computers and connections, with different browsers and maybe different operating systems. Maybe they are viewing it on a 3G mobile phone? Perhaps they have poor eyesight and want to enlarge the fonts, or are even severely visually impaired and rely on a screen reader. If you adhere to HTML, CSS and Accessibility standards you will be catering for all of the above, and much more. You are also future-proofing your site, making it easier to update the structure in the future.

If a human can access your site better, then so can an automated search engine robot, which needs to be able to read accurate code in order to categorise its content. If there are fundamental errors in your code such as broken links, then any search engine will have problems. Google does state that it 'prefers clean, compliant code'; although the general consensus in the SEO community is that minor errors should not have a detrimental effect on your rankings.

9. Getting Links to Your Site

By this stage, you should have a lightweight, compliant site with plenty of fresh, optimised content. So search engines are going to immediately rank you at number 1, right? Probably not! While you've certainly made the site a friendly place for them when they arrive, they need a good reason to go there. In the next chapter, we will cover what you need to do to tell search engines about your site, but even more important than that is to get other sites linking into yours.

Search engines place a great deal of importance on the quality of links rather than simply sheer numbers of links. If you sell golf clubs and can get various high-ranking golfing sites to link to you, then this will dramatically improve your rankings. When a user searches for a term, search engines scour their databases for sites that contain the term in question, and then apply various filters, such as 'is the term in the page title', 'is it in a hyperlink to the page' etc – most of these have been covered in previous chapters. One of the first filters it will apply when assigning a position to a results page is whether the page in question has quality links coming into it.

Checking the number of links into your site
It is surprisingly easy to see which sites link to you from most search engines. Simply type in link:www.yourdomainname.com into a search and you will see a list of all of the pages that are linking to you. So, of course the next step is to repeat this exercise with all of your competitors, and identify the major sites that you may be able to get a link from.

If you want to get a quick idea of the number of links into yours and your competitor sites, then try the fabulous (and of course free) Link Popularity Check, available from www.checkyourlinkpopularity.com. Enter in as many URLs as you wish and you can get an immediate comparison of the number of links into each site by five major search engines. Double-clicking on any of the specific search engine totals will perform the same function as demonstrated in the previous paragraph, listing all sites that link into your site.

Getting More Visitors to Your Website in 90 Minutes

9.1 Link Popularity Check shows you how many sites link to yours.

Swapping links

The first place to look for incoming links is through the people you know. This generally falls into three categories: customers, suppliers and complimenting businesses/web sites. Create a links page on your site and offer an exchange of links between your site and theirs. Explain the benefits that they will achieve by doing this.

Agree to be a case study for your suppliers in exchange for a link back to your site – you'll also get some great free PR out of it as they will no doubt paint you as a forward-thinking, dynamic company that is benefiting from using their product/service. If you are already writing case studies on your customers, ask for a reciprocal link (as no doubt you are already linking to them).

If you have any mutually beneficial relationships with vendors serving the same customer base (but not selling the same products), see if you can get links from their sites. Remember: by getting links from sites that are also in your industry, search engines will treat these as more important than a link from a site that has no relevance to yours.

Getting Links to Your Site

Become a voice on discussion groups
Back in chapter 2, we discussed the merit of adding a **forum** to your site, but you can also use other forums to your benefit. Find forums that are relevant to your industry and 'lurk'. Lurking is the term used to describe people that visit the forums but don't post. You won't be lurking for long, however. If people are posting questions that you can answer on a professional level then do so, but make sure that underneath your name you put a link back to your site. When search engines spider their site they will find these links and follow them back. If that site carries weight with the search engines (e.g. it is a large, respected and busy site) then this link has more value to you – the more links across other sites of a similar quality you can get, the better.

You may also have heard of **newsgroups**. These are pretty much identical to the forums described above in that they are 'virtual rooms' that people can meet in to discuss relevant topics, although the mechanism used to read/reply is different. Newsgroups started way back in 1979 in an academic environment and until the early nineties were mainly used by students and those with software-related interests. Nowadays there are some 60,000 newsgroups available, and there are probably several that are specific to key areas of your industry. Newsgroups use an infrastructure called Usenet, whereas bulletin boards appear on standard web pages. While Usenet itself is not spidered by many search engines, Google Groups (formerly Déjà Vu) does spider and archive news threads.

A newsgroup can be described as 'public, threaded email'. You can use programs such as Outlook Express to read newsgroup postings in much the same way that you read emails, except you will see a 'tree' where the thread of replies grows. You will need to speak to your ISP to find their news server address so that you can create a new account in Outlook Express.

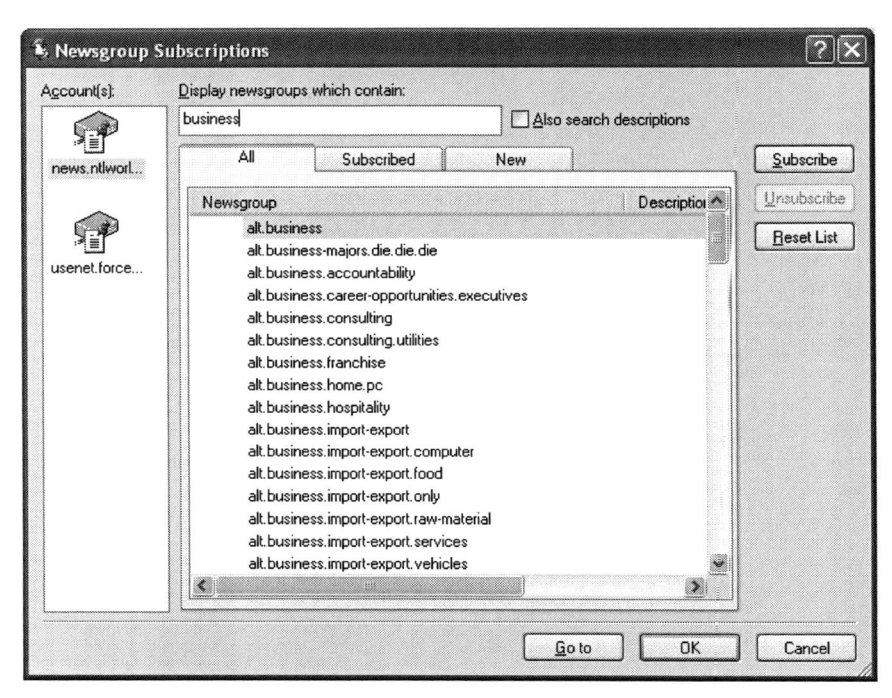

9.2. Usenet newsgroups can also be an excellent way of spreading links, as Google Groups will spider them

Important: It is very easy to be drawn into a slanging match in forums, where a disgruntled user or competitor starts criticising your product or company and you feel it necessary to defend yourself. Avoid this at all costs. If it is a popular site and your postings contain relevant keywords then it is highly possible that such a page would get high rankings – perhaps even higher rankings than your own site!

PR, PR and more PR

Earlier we mentioned case studies as a way of generating PR. It is important to maintain a regular press presence in general, which can cover anything from news on new staff appointments to product releases and updates. Most printed media now have a website to match, where they will post news as soon as they get it. Most will also link back to your site for free, although some will sell this as an additional service. Depending on the importance of the title it may be worth paying for – usually it is just a nominal fee per year. Magazine sites are especially important to appear on, as search engines

Getting Links to Your Site

generally rank them high due to the large amount of fresh content that appears to them. There are some 'e-zines' available – these are electronic-only magazines, and as a result they tend to generate much more content more quickly than their traditional counterparts. They may also print longer articles, as they are not constrained by space and see the benefit in the additional content – they will often take anything you can send their way!

Finding more sites

After you've covered your own contact database, it is time to widen the net. While you could just trawl the web in search of similar sites, as luck would have it there is yet another tool that will automate the task for you. From the same people that brought you the Link Popularity Check program covered earlier comes Arelis. This is a paid-for application that helps you to find prospective partnering sites, and provides an automated method of contacting them and tracking their response. It will also build reciprocal link pages for you to place on your site.

Using Arelis to build a link swapping campaign

Download the free trial version for starters. Then enter the keywords that you have selected for your site. Arelis will then search for similar sites and provide the resulting sites in a list. You can then modify parameters for each site, such as whether you will include a link back from your site to theirs, which category/subcategory they will be listed in on your site, their weight (importance) etc. Once you have defined all of the relevant prospective sites, you can customise the emails that it can automatically deliver.

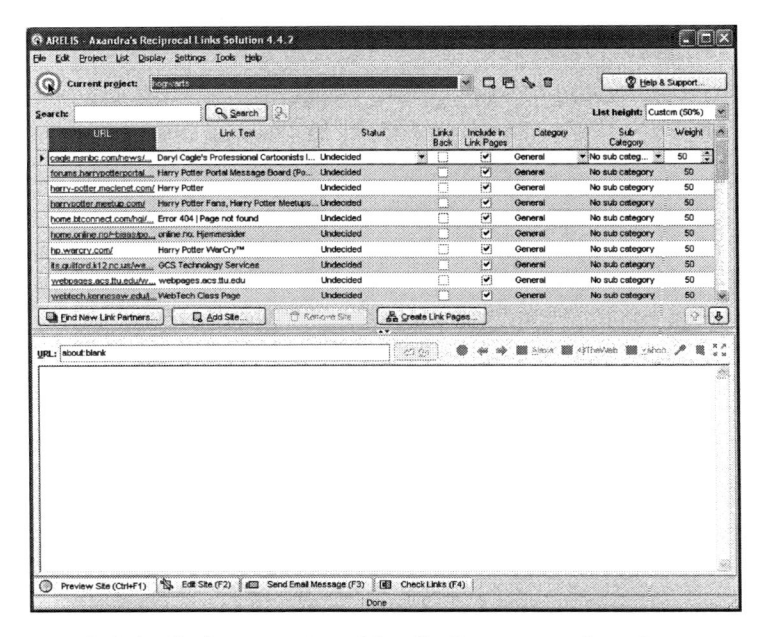

9.3 Arelis is a great tool for finding partnering sites

Syndicating your content

Earlier we discussed adding technical articles to your site. If these are relatively 'vanilla' e.g. they are not focusing on your product or service but lean more towards a general fact sheet, then you might want to consider syndicating your content. Put simply this means allowing other sites to publish your articles as long as they link back to your site. To find suitable syndication partners do a search for 'syndicate article' plus a keyword relevant to your industry – no doubt you will find a site that specialises in hosting articles in your field. One general site is articlecity.com, which accepts articles on subjects as diverse as trucks, pets and religion.

Getting Links to Your Site

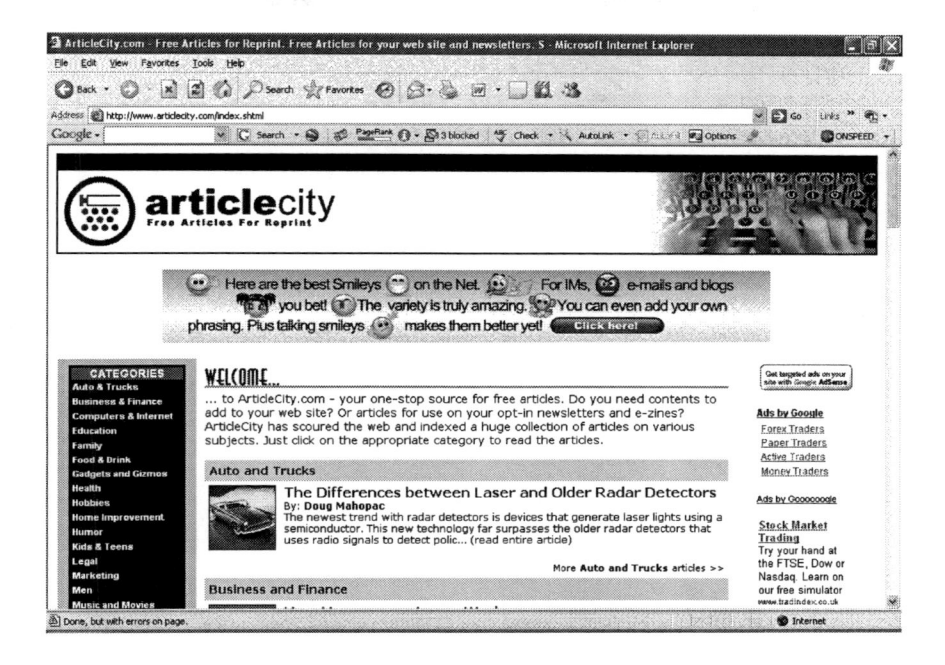

9.4. Articlecity is just one of many good content syndication sites available

Why should you give your content away? Sites such as these not only host a large amount of content, but they also allow all articles to be taken and re-used as long as credit and a link goes back to the author. Therefore if you are providing something of value – your content – you will get a link back to your site in return. And as anyone looking to take content from sites such as this is likely to be in your industry, you are virtually guaranteed a quality link back into your site.

> **Summary**
> Without links into your site, it will always be seen as a minnow in comparison to some of the larger fish in your industrial pond. Syndicating your content is a great way of spreading the word, making yourself a voice in the industry and getting more high quality links in. Keep an eye on how you stand with in-bound links in comparison to your competitors, and place more importance on finding new quality links if you are behind them.

10. Using Content from Other Websites

In addition to providing others with your content, you can also use content from other sites as a tool to bring visitors to yours. RSS – Really Simple Syndication – is a technology that has only recently broken into the mainstream. Sites such as www.bbc.co.uk allow anyone to take information such as live news headlines and either read them locally or even display them on their own site. RSS uses a file format called XML – eXtensible Markup Language.

10.1 Sites such as the BBC allow you to place their content on your site.

So what can RSS do for you?

Simple – it can provide free and regularly updated content that requires

73

minimal effort from you. It might be suitable to have several RSS feeds, each covering different topics. You can browse to any of the section on the BBC's news service and use the headlines as a basis for a 'feed' on your own. These could be as diverse as the latest e-commerce news, or the latest premiership football headlines.

RSS can be displayed on your site in a variety of different ways, but the best way is to use one of the many RSS to HTML converters. These (often free) scripts automate the process of creating a page which is dynamically created with the latest headlines each time a user visits the page. One such script is available at www.feeddigest.com. There are many other scripts available that work in a similar fashion, so feel free to check out the competition. The interesting part for us is the way in which we embed these feeds into our site – it is done in such a way that when visitors and search engines alike visit your page, they will both see the content taken from the other site as if it were on yours. This is the key – assuming you choose a site with relevant topics, the resulting page will update frequently and be rich in keywords.

Creating a feed that embeds the content in your site
Within a few minutes of finishing this chapter you could easily have generated a page on your website that is rich in keywords and has fresh, automated content. For this technique to work you must have the ability to run PHP scripts – a service that most ISPs provide as standard or for a small fee.

Let's say that you want to add a news feed page on your site specific to UK Business. We can take this further and add several feeds covering various niche topics within this heading.

Step 1 – find an RSS feed
The first stage is to find your site (or sites) that provide their content for syndication. We mentioned the BBC site, so for now we'll use that. Go to http://news.bbc.co.uk and select Business from the left-hand menu. Towards the bottom of the menu you will see an orange RSS logo. Click on this – the page that follows will contain the code you will be using. Copy the URL from the web browser address bar to the clipboard (by selecting it and pressing CTRL & C).

Using Content from Other Websites

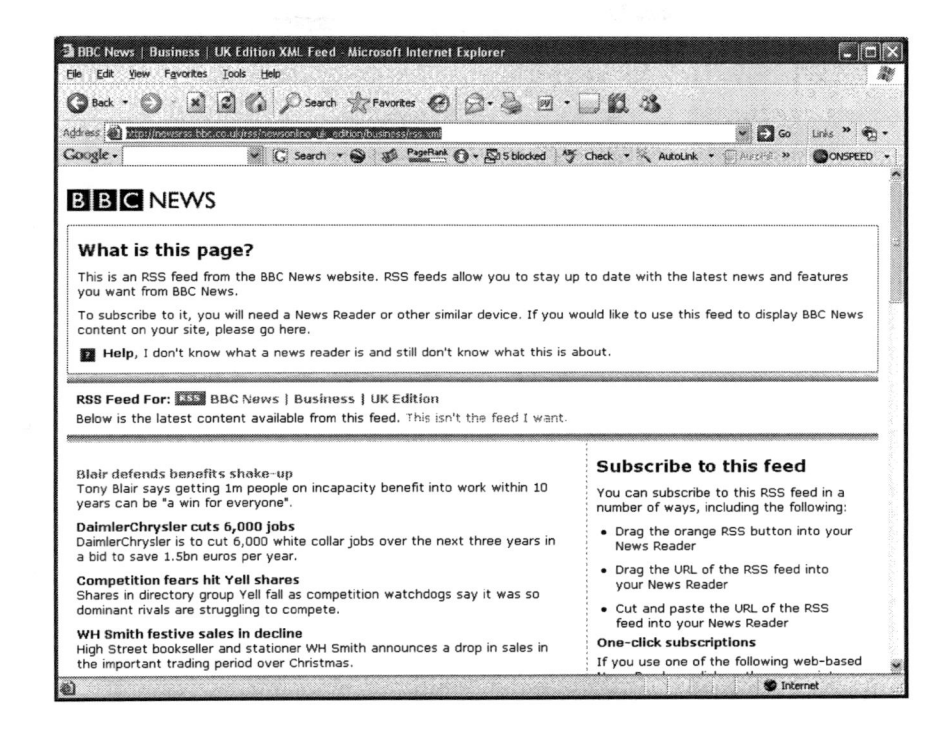

10.2. The first step is to find your RSS feed

Step 2 – Create an account on Feeddigest.com

Point a web browser to www.feeddigest.com and paste the URL into the long field under the 'Sign up here' text. A basic account is free and allows up to 5 'digests' (groups of feeds), each of which can have 5 sources. On the next page the news feed is verified and you can format the output. Formatting options include number of items, order of items and several template layouts. You can even add other feeds to this to get a good mix of sources. After selecting your template, the following page will provide you with your feed in a variety of formats – it's the HTML one that we are interested in. Click on the HTML output link and copy the URL from the popup window that appears.

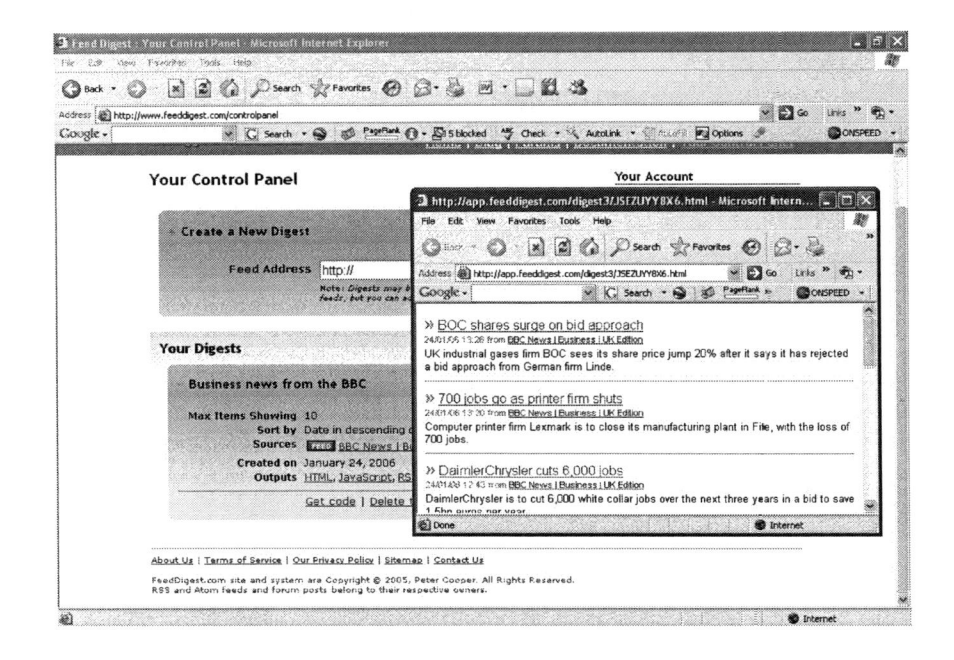

10.3. Within minutes you have your RSS feed

Step 3 – Adding the code to your site

Create a new page based on your usual web page template, or open the page you want to insert the feed. You now need to add in code similar to below, changing the URL in bold to the one you copied from step 2.

<?php

include ('http://app.feeddigest.com/digest3/XXXX.html');

?>

Save your page, upload it and open it in a web browser – you should see your newsfeed inserted neatly within your usual page style.

Using Content from Other Websites

> **Summary**
>
> RSS feeds are a great way to seamlessly embed fresh content into your site, keeping both visitors and search engines happy while reducing your own workload.

11. Submitting Your Site to Search Engines

Once you've got this far, the rest is technically very easy – in fact if you already have good quality links coming into your site you will probably find that Google and the like are happily harvesting your content.

Before you submit your site to search engines, make sure that you have followed the optimisation techniques covered in this book – don't submit first and then tweak your site. Submitting a poorly optimised, bloated and potentially error-laden site can work against you, especially if it contains unnoticed elements that could get you blacklisted.

Submitting your site to search engines is simply a matter of going to the relevant site, finding the Submit Site/URL link and entering the required information. For Google this is http://www.google.com/addurl/?continue=/addurl

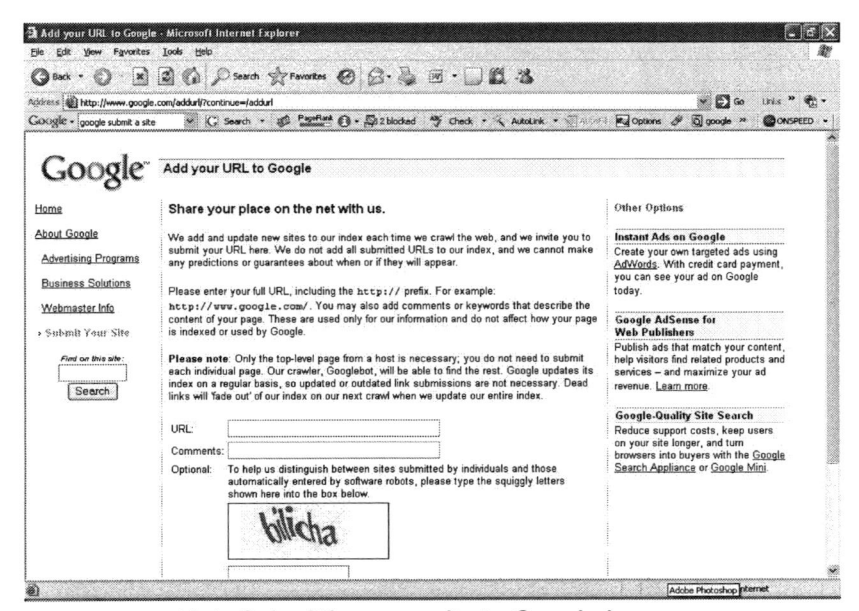

11.1. Submitting your site to Google is easy

Getting More Visitors to Your Website in 90 Minutes

To find the relevant page per search engine, either look for the link somewhere on the page (Yahoo has 'How to suggest a site' at the bottom of its page) or simply do a search with 'suggest URL' and the search engine name.

This is, of course quite a laborious process and as you would expect there are ways to automate it. A quick search for 'search engine submission software' will throw up a multitude of products. One of the leaders is Apex Pacific's 'Dynamic' product range – both web-based and local PC software based search engine optimisation submission systems.

Dynamic Submission is a program that is installed on your PC. It has a database of thousands of web sites, broken down by country and category – you can download updated databases to ensure you are submitting to the latest engines. You start by creating a profile, followed by selecting the categories/search engines that are relevant to you. The software can also create Meta tags based on your chosen keywords, and provide you with an assessment of your page based upon these keywords. Once done, you click on submit, and then go and make a coffee while it submits your site(s) to your chosen engines automatically.

Dynamic SEO Manager effectively does the same job, but has the benefit of being controlled by a web browser.

Submitting Your Site to Search Engines

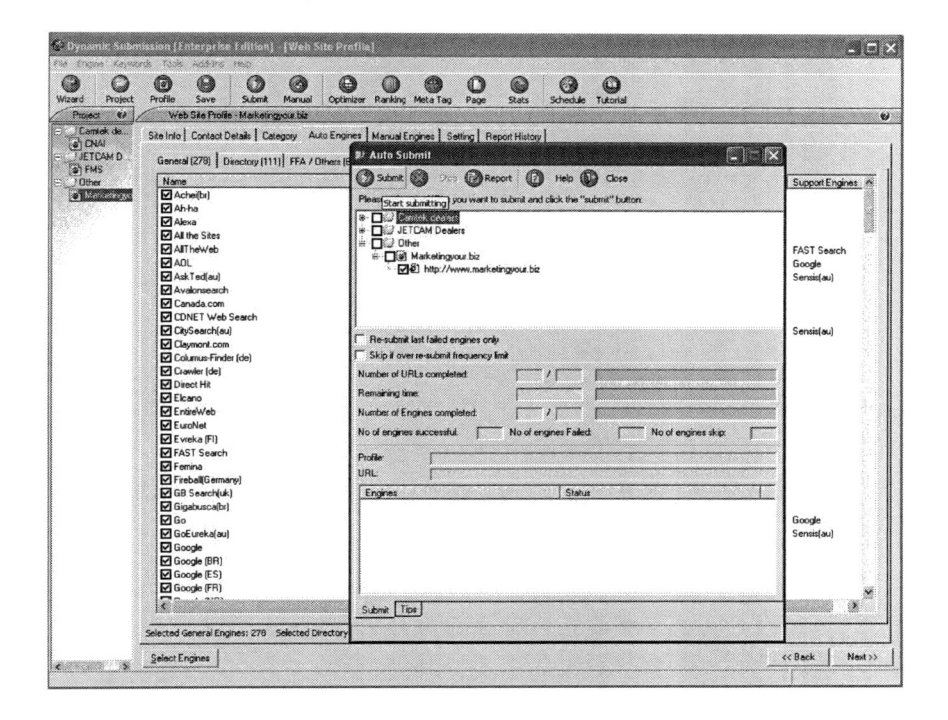

11.2. You can easily automate the submission process if you are prepared to pay.

Note: WebCEO also has a search engine submission tool within its free version that will automatically submit to several hundred sites. The process is similar to Dynamic Submission, so try both to see which one suits your needs best.

Important: You can over-submit your site to search engines. Google recommends leaving at least 4-6 weeks between submissions.

Summary

While it may seem strange that the search engine submission chapter appears near the end of this book it is important to understand that this is one of the last processes in the chain - once you submit your site and it (hopefully) gets listed, it is then a case of continuing to feed content into your site and monitor its success.

Submit your site to search engines within a 1-2 month period, but not more frequently as this can work against you. If you are doing everything else right then this task should take a lower priority in your to-do list.

12. Tracking Your Effectiveness Through Web Statistics

Many people feel isolated from their website once it is live – it's not like a shop or a factory that you can physically keep watch over. Not so! There are plenty of tools that can allow you to track who visits your site and what they do when they get there. It is also important to check that the optimisation techniques that you employ are effective so that you can take action quickly if they don't.

Let's dispel one question that I am still occasionally asked: there is no way that you can automatically collect the email address of everyone who visits your site! But there are still many useful pieces of information that you can extract and analyse, such as:

- whether the person typed in your web address or whether they clicked on a link to your site
- which search engine they used to find you
- which keywords they used within the search engine
- what page they landed on, and the subsequent path they took through your site
- information about their computer, such as browser, screen resolution, rough geographical location etc.

This information is normally totalised and sorted in descending order, so you might choose to look at the top 10 pages, followed by the top 10 keywords or phrases used to locate your site.

There are various ways that you can analyse this information. You can either analyse log files that are usually stored on your server or add some code to your pages that allow a third party to perform the same task.

Your first port of call should be to your ISP to check that (a) they store your log files on your server (usually in a folder called logs, logfiles or stats), and (b) that they install/provide one of the many free online and instant web analysis tools available – AWStats, Webalizer and Analog are three of the more common tools. These tools allow you to get reports with either live or recent data by visiting a web page within your site – usually in a password protected sub-folder.

If none of these applications is installed on your web space, it is not overly difficult to get them working. All of them have comprehensive instructions on their homepages and most ISPs will be able to lend a hand (assuming they don't want to lose your business to a host that provides stats ready to run).

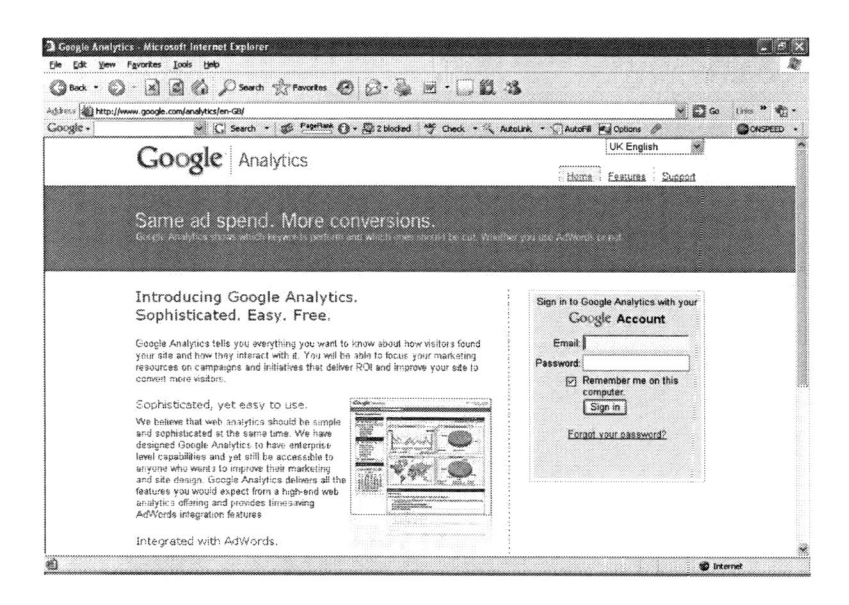

12.1 Google Analytics

Google Analytics

Analysing your logs on your server is your first option, although there are other companies that will monitor your site, the most notable of which is the omnipresent Google. Formerly known as Urchin and charged at $200 per month, Google now provides its Analytics service free of charge. This web-based analysis system provides site owners with traffic metrics and useful marketing data. Analytics integrates with Google's popular AdWords banner advertising system, and will vastly improve the quality and quantity of data provided to existing AdWords users. Google are not giving this service out of the kindness of their hearts. The free version is limited to sites with 5 million page views per month – enough for a great many sites, however AdWords customers get unlimited page view analysis.

If you don't use AdWords you can still use Analytics by adding a simple JavaScript snippet to the <HEAD> section of your template. By doing this all pages based on it will be tracked. To get Google Analytics checking your site follow these steps:

1. Goto www.google.com/analytics/ and register (or use an AdWords or Gmail username/password
2. Copy the code that Google provides, and then open up your web template. Paste the code just before the end </HEAD> tag. Save the template and upload all pages that are updated by the template
3. Google will take 24-48 hours to update your stats – once done you'll be able to harvest the fruits of your efforts

Offline analysis

For many people, these online tools are more than adequate. However, if you want to dig deeper, then you might want to consider downloading your log files and using a program to analyse the files locally.

If your ISP stores log files on your server, they are generally in a folder called stats or logs, with files ending in .log or .gz. You will need to download these using your FTP software and store them in a folder for processing locally.

A great free tool for this purpose is Weblog Expert Lite, available at http://www.weblogexpert.com/lite.htm. A full version is also available; however the free version does provide valuable information such as referring sites, top search engines and key phrases, top pages and files along with top errors.

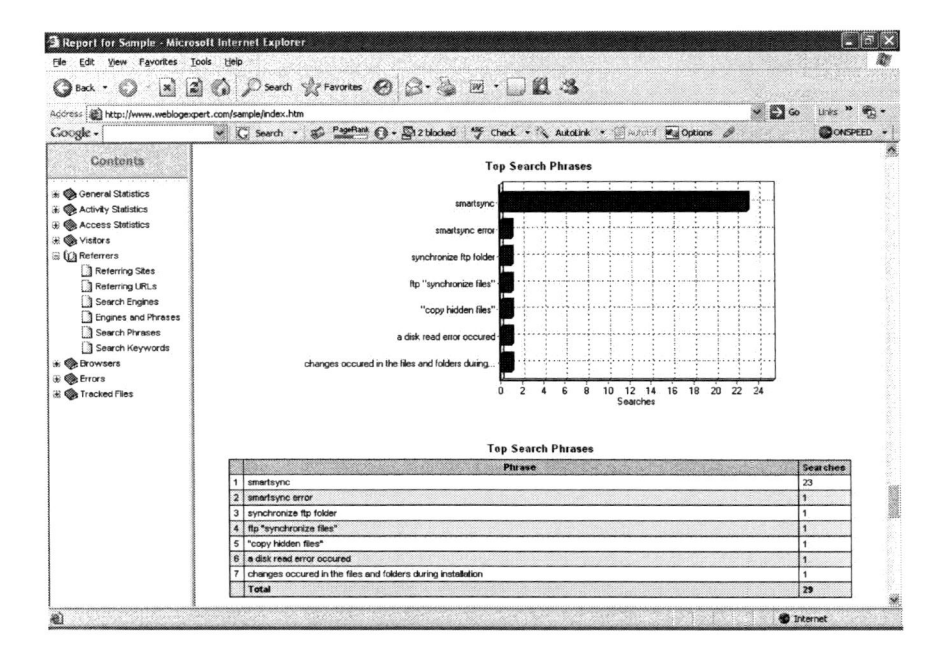

12.2 Weblog Expert Lite provides excellent and free statistical analysis

So why should you install Weblog Expert Lite (or, god forbid buy the full version) when Google provides you analysis for free? Well, Google's information covers some areas very well and others very sketchily. Error reporting is non-existent (at the time of writing). Therefore the best way forward is to cover all bases – use Google Analytics weekly to keep an eye on things, and use an offline analysis tool monthly to dig deeper.

Tracking Your Effectiveness Through Web Statistics

> **Summary**
> Keeping an eye on your logs is the equivalent of checking the showroom after the customers have had a look around. You can see who's been where and what areas are of interest. You can see what is not working well or, more importantly, not at all. Site statistics give you a finger on the pulse of how your efforts are paying off and should play a regular part in your site maintenance. There are plenty of free or low-cost tools that will provide you all of the stats you need.

13. Offline Promotion

Promoting your website does not stop when you switch your computer off. There are a number of things that you can do to drive people to your site.

Leave your mark
Anything that leaves your offices should carry your web address. This includes invoices, letterheads, envelopes, newsletters, case studies, press releases etc. If you have a shop front or building sign make sure that your web address is visible to passing traffic – if your URL is your company name then you could even make this the main visual element of your logo.

Mobile web address
For companies that have a fleet of vehicles, they can be used as mobile billboards, although for sales reps you may wish to limit this to a discrete rear window sticker.

Word of mouth
Ensure that all of your staff are familiar with the site and its content, and refer to it during conversations. When updates are made to it, make sure that you communicate this to them. They can use the site as a first line of contact – for customers wanting immediate information staff can either point them to relevant sections or email links from the site to them.

Freebies
Everybody loves something for nothing. Pens, USB memory sticks, mouse mats, mugs, coasters, calendars etc. These are often given out to customers after a sale, at trade shows or at Christmas. These days, all you really need to print on them is your name, web address and phone number (unless space permits more).

You can use services such as CafePress.com to create a wide range of products that you use as promotional items, or even set up your own store to sell your branded products online! Note that this is predominantly a US site, but there are country-specific alternatives.

Getting More Visitors to Your Website in 90 Minutes

13.1. Create your own branded products in low quantities

Adverts

Any advertising should feature your web address as prominently as your phone number. Your adverts can also be used as a 'call to action' to drive people specifically to the site for web-only offers.

Offline Promotion

Summary
Your website is a means for your customers to access information about your business 24/7. While the other chapters concentrate on driving online prospects to your site through you still have to consider those that are interacting with you offline. Maybe they haven't found you during their time online or perhaps have yet to make the leap into cyberspace. In short, you need to ensure that every method that you use to interact with customers offline makes them aware of your online presence. Where your phone number would have appeared 10 years ago, ensure that your web address appears alongside or even instead of.

Appendix 1: Quick Checklist

Below is a summary of what you should be doing to get and keep your site in tip-top condition for both search engines and visitors alike.

- ✓ Ensure that you add new content regularly – search engines prefer sites that have 'fresh meat'.
- ✓ The more content you can add, the better.
- ✓ Get valid! Validate your HTML and CSS code to check that it is accurate. Ideally convert it to the newer XHTML coding standard.
- ✓ Test your site in different browsers and resolutions, especially after any major changes. If possible, check on different systems (such as Mac and Unix).
- ✓ Make your site as accessible as possible – run your site through accessibility validators regularly.
- ✓ Send out PR regularly to printed and online magazines, ensuring that your web address is clearly marked in the release.
- ✓ Add a standard site map page to your site to help visitors.
- ✓ Add a Google sitemap to your site, and update it regularly, or automate the updating process through a script.
- ✓ Be on the constant lookout for sites that will link to you – provide reciprocal links where applicable.
- ✓ Resubmit your site to search engines ever 1-2 months – not too frequently or you may get blacklisted for spamming.
- ✓ Check your web stats regularly to ensure that there are no errors (such as 404 – page not found) and to see what is working and what is not.

Appendix 2: Google's Most Loved and Hated SEO Tricks

While this is not information that Google publishes, there are many heated exchanges in SEO forums worldwide that have reached some interesting conclusions, which have been compiled below. Note that these are of course subject to change! Note also that some of the factors listed in the Positive section can work against you if your site jumps to the negative list, perhaps because you fell foul of another factor.

Positive factors

1. Keyword in URL
2. Keyword in domain name
3. Head: Keyword in title tag
4. Head: Keyword in description meta tag
5. Head: Keyword in keyword meta tag
6. Body: Keyword density – should be over 5% but do not go over 20%
7. Body: Keyword in H1, H2 or H3
8. Body: Keyword font size (bold, italics, etc)
9. Body: Keyword proximity (e.g. where two keywords are close to each other)
10. Size and age of page/site

Negative factors

1. Text in graphic form only, leaving no content within the body
2. Don't be an affiliate site with 'all link and no content'
3. Linking to link farms or a blacklisted site – you will get tarred with the same brush
4. Redirecting through REFRESH Meta tags
5. Vile language or putting normal words together that can have a different meaning. In fact anything that can be deemed offensive, including racial or ethnic slurs

6. Excessive cross links, especially within the same IP block (suggesting the same server)
7. Keyword stuffing – keep keywords to a sensible level
8. Using frames – even now search engines have problems with frames
9. Invisible text (e.g. same as background colour). Also, very small text
10. Gateway pages

Appendix 3 – The Web Promoter's Software Arsenal

There are several software applications that no site promoter should be without. While there are many applications available that perform the similar functions, each have their own merits and are worthy of space on your hard disc. All of these are either free or have a trial or cut-down version available.

Arelis Reciprocal Links finder
Searches out potential sites to swap links with. Also creates emails that can be sent automatically to all prospective sites and helps to manage responses. Excellent for getting quality links back into your site.

Trial version available from www.axandra.com.

Dynamic Submission
Enterprise standard site submission tool. Provides a downloadable database of 10,000+ search engines to ensure that you submit to current engines.

Demo version available at www.dynamicsubmission.com

Link Popularity Check
Allows you to enter yours and your competitors URLS and see how many pages are linking into you. Checks against AllTheWeb, Altavista, Google/Hotbot, MSN Search, Teoma and Yahoo.

Free version available from www.checkyourlinkpopularity.com.

Mozilla FireFox
The biggest threat to Microsoft's stranglehold on the web browser market since the days of Netscape. Firefox is open source and free. There are also many free plugins available. All sites should be tested in Firefox as well as IE.

Free download from www.firefox.org.

Opera
Trailing behind Firefox as the third most popular browser, this is a lightweight, fully functional and extremely fast browser. While it will

probably only account for less than 5% of your visitors it is still worth checking your pages with it.

Free download from www.opera.com.

SiteDigger
Although not strictly a web promotion tool, this free application will identify potential security problems with your site, using a list of known flaws and attack methods.

Free version available from www.foundstone.com.

Vigos Gsitemap generator
Free tool to generate a Google Sitemap. Automatically creates the complex Google XML file that helps the goliath search engine to find your fresh content.

Available online at www.vigos.com.

WebCEO
Covers all of the main requirements: Researching keywords, optimising pages, editing pages (although you are better off doing this in your regular editor), submitting to search engines, checking your rankings against keywords and competitors, and analysing your link popularity. A number of paid-for services are also available.

Free version available from www.webceo.com.

Weblog Expert
Excellent offline log file analysis. Two versions are available – Lite and Full. The Lite version provides basic, but adequate stats information for most.

Free version available from www.weblogexpert.com.

Appendix 4 – Useful Sites

www.adwordsmarket.com/
Alternative to Google's Sandbox and Overtures keyword information tools.

www.alexa.com
This site provides information about site traffic and links from other sites. Useful for finding information on sites that link to you and their influence on search engines.

www.analogx.com
Site that offers a variety of tools, including Keyword Live, which allows you to analyse how often a keyword is used on a website – great for checking to see why your competitors rank higher than you in search engines!

www.arelis.com
Software that searches for non-competing sites that you can link to and request links from, thus increasing your traffic and search engine popularity.

www.hitbox.com
Providers of online website statistics, including Hitbox personal, a free service.

www.maxreferrer.com
A web-based referral system allowing you to let visitors recommend your site to others, inform them of special announcements and invite them to sign up for newsletters. An ideal tool for viral marketing on the web.

www.rlrouse.com
21 step guide to getting top rankings in Google and Yahoo.

www.robotstxt.org
Information on how to create a robots.txt file for your website.

www.searchenginewatch.com
Site focusing on news on the latest search engine developments.

www.webconfs.com/
A site hosting a number of search engine optimisation tools, such as search engine spider simulator, similar page checker and keyword density checker.

www.webmasterworld.com
Site offering in-depth search engine optimisation advice, along with building and marketing tips.

Glossary of Terms

AJAX Asynchronous JavaScript and XML. A new method of programming that replaces the traditional 'click submit' approach of passing data. A good example of this is Google Suggest, which suggests search keywords as you type each letter.

Blog basically a journal that is available on the web. The activity of updating a blog is 'blogging' and someone who keeps a blog is a 'blogger.' Blogs are typically updated daily using software that allows people with little or no technical background to update and maintain the blog. Postings on a blog are almost always arranged in chronological order with the most recent additions featured most prominently. Blogger.com is the most well-known.

Case Study a document that details information about one of your customers, detailing why they chose you and the benefits/savings they have achieved due to your products/services. Can also be used as a press release.

CSS Cascading Style Sheets. Used within web pages to maintain a common look and feel across all pages. Once a CSS document is created, all font sizes, styles and colours are defined in one place, allowing all pages to be updated from one source.

Domain A domain name is used rather than an IP address (a string of numbers) to locate a website.

FTP File Transfer Protocol. The name used for the software that transfers files between your computer and a web server.

GIF Graphic file format mainly used for images on web sites. Is limited to 256 colours or less – decreasing the number of colours reduces the file size, so can result in a very graphical page that can load very quickly.

HTML HyperText Markup Language. The language structure that founded the web.

ISP	Internet Service Provider. A company that provides you with access to the internet, either through dial-up or ADSL/Cable modem (broadband).
JPG	(pronounced Jay-Peg and also known as JPEG). Graphic file format mainly used for pictures on web sites due to its high compression ratios, which result in small file sizes.
Newsgroup	An electronic discussion group allowing you to post messages that others can see and reply to, building a 'thread' of messages linked by a common subject. Newsgroups are generally free to subscribe to.
Open Source	Software that is not only free, but the source code is also openly available for modification and development. The Linux operating system, OpenOffice suite, Joomla CMS and SugarSuite CRM systems are good examples of this.
Rollover	term used to describe a graphic or text that will change when the cursor rolls over it.
RSS	Really Simple Syndication. A method of allowing others to show your web content on their site.
SEF	A web page that conforms to most guidelines laid down by the Search Engines for web page creation and which does not breach any Terms of Inclusion in a Search Engine.
SEM	Search Engine Marketing. Locating, researching, submitting, and positioning a website within the proper search engines for maximum exposure and effectiveness. SEM may also include the function of choosing the target keywords and keyword phrases for the website's meta tags.
SEO	Search Engine Optimisation. Many web submission companies now call themselves 'SEO Experts'. Also referred to as SEM (Search Engine Marketing).
URL	Unique Resource Location. Term used to describe a web address. Usually starts with http://
W3C	The official body of standards for the Internet.
WYSIWYG	What You See Is What You Get. Term used to describe

Appendices

	applications that display on-screen what will be output to a different media e.g. printer. A good example is a Word Processor.
XHTML	eXtensible Hypertext Markup Language. The successor to HTML, which allows integration with XML (such as RSS newsfeeds)
XML	(Extensible Markup Language) is a W3C initiative that allows information and services to be encoded with meaningful structure and semantics that computers and humans can understand. XML is great for information exchange, and can easily be extended to include user-specified and industry-specified tags. RSS uses XML extensively.

Index

'A NAME' records, 45
Accessibility, 61
Adverts, 90
ALT text, 43
Analog Keyword Extractor, 41
Archie, 9
Arelis, 69
Articlecity, 71
Author, 29

Bulletin boards, 15

Cascading Style Sheets, 33
Case studies, 15
Checking for errors, 57
Clean up HTML, 58
CMS system, 50, 60
Common errors, 56
Compliancy, 55
Content, 43
Content is King, 15
Content Management System, 50
Copyright, 29
CSS, 33

Dead links, 56
Description, 27
Directories, 10
Discussion forums, 15
  groups, 67
Domain name, 12, 44
Dreamweaver, 35, 55
Dynamic Submission, 80

Effectiveness, 83

Excite, 9

Feeddigest.com 75
File names, 42
Firefox, 55
Flash, 17, 18
Forum, 16, 67
Freebies, 89

Google, 10
Google Analytics, 84
  Sandbox, 22
  site map, 51
Gopher, 9

Heart Internet, 46
History, 9
Homepage, 28
HTML Code, 33
HTML vs XHTML, 55
Hyperlink 'title' text, 44
Hyperlink text, 43

Indexing, 18
Internet Explorer, 55
Intro screens, 18
IP address, 12

JavaScript code, 37

Keyword Effectiveness Index, 24
Keywords, 21, 27, 41

Link Popularity Check, 65
Links, 65

Index

Log files, 83

Meta search engines, 10
Meta tags, 27
Minors, 28
Mobile web address, 89
mySQL database, 15

Nesting tags, 56
Newsgroups, 67

Offline analysis, 85
  approach, 21
  promotion, 89
Online approach, 21
  forums, 15
Opera, 55
Optimised domain name, 45
Optimising the site, 41
Other websites, 73
Overture, 22
Overview, 9
Own branded products, 90

Page title, 42
Pay per Click, 10
phpBB, 15
PR, 68
  content, 15
Pragma, 28

Quick checklist, 93

Rating, 28
Really Simple Syndication, 73
Revisit-after, 29
Robots, 29

RSS feed, 74

Sandbox, 21
Screen resolutions, 62
Search engine, 9, 79
  types, 10
Shockwave, 17
Site maps, 49
Spiders, 18
Streamlining, 33
Submitting site, 79
Suggest, 22
Swapping links, 66
Syndicating, 70

Tables, 57
Template problems, 60
Testing, 62
Text, 15

URL problems, 60

Valid code, 58
Validation, 60

W3C, 55
W3C valid code page, 59
WebCEO, 24, 42, 47
Web statistics, 83
Weblog Expert Lite, 85
WebXact, 62
Word of mouth, 89
Wordtracker, 23
World Wide Web Consortium, 55

Zen Garden, 34

Notes and Ideas

Notes and Ideas

Notes and Ideas

Notes and Ideas

Notes and Ideas